Michael Hill

TOUGHEN UP

what I've learned about surviving tough times

with Claire Harvey

RANDOM HOUSE
NEW ZEALAND

With thanks to Claire Harvey

A RANDOM HOUSE BOOK published by Random House New Zealand
18 Poland Road, Glenfield, Auckland, New Zealand
For more information about our titles go to www.randomhouse.co.nz

A catalogue record for this book is available from the National Library of New Zealand

Random House New Zealand is part of the Random House Group
New York London Sydney Auckland Delhi Johannesburg

First published 2009
© Michael Hill 2009
The moral rights of the author have been asserted
ISBN 978 1 86979 046 2

Random House New Zealand uses non chlorine-bleached papers from sustainably managed plantation forests.
Design: Monika Hill
Cover photograph: Mark Hill
Printed in Australia by Griffin Press

I dedicate this book to you,
because you *can* do it.

ILLUSTRATED BY MICHAEL HILL

CONTENTS

There is only one boss
— the customer. He
fires everybody simply
by spending his money
somewhere else.

Sam Walton

Introduction

Recession, depression, collapse, chaos. We might as well all give up now. This is a terrible time for business.

That, I am sorry to say, is the common wisdom of today. Everywhere I hear pundits saying the financial world is in turmoil, businesses are failing, entrepreneurship is doomed.

I don't believe it for a second — and I would like to show you why.

Over the years, I have had just about every possible experience in business: from lie-awake-at-night nerves to the joy of unexpected success. I've reshaped the landscape under my feet and I have ventured into new territory. And at every moment, I have relished the excitement of it all. Even during the difficult times — and there have been plenty

Top: Me as a baby, with my mother, Billie, circa 1939. Bottom: Spearfishing at the Poor Knights Islands, northern New Zealand, 1959.

— I've been conscious that all this is an incredible adventure, a voyage of exploration that I'm extraordinarily lucky to be on.

Once, I was an outsider in my industry, the cheeky start-up whom nobody expected to succeed. The established players had no reason to view me as a threat.

Now, my business is the establishment. We dominate the markets in which we operate. Michael Hill Jeweller is a respected part of the business culture in a large part of the world — and we are continuing to expand in both size and ambition.

I was born in 1938 in the north of New Zealand, in Whangarei, where I learned the art of sales from my father Dickie Hill, who worked in the jewellery shop owned by his brother-in-law, my uncle Arthur Fisher. For 23 years I too worked in the shop, selling jewels to the townsfolk and never daring to speak aloud my quiet ambition: to one day buy the business and run it as my own. I hadn't the first idea how to make my dream a reality; my uncle did not like me much, and had no intention of allowing his precious business to pass into my hands.

So I busied myself with the ordinary joys of life. I married a beautiful Englishwoman, Christine, and we had two children, Mark and Emma. We spent the weekends sailing and fishing, and devoted ourselves to building our own home overlooking the gleaming harbour. As the years rolled on, I found it easier and easier to avoid thinking about my dream — owning the shop seemed a faraway impossibility.

Then, in a single night, everything went up in smoke — literally. Our house burnt to the ground. Standing amid the soggy ashes of my house, looking at my little family with nothing but the clothes on our backs, my life changed for ever. 'I will buy my uncle's business,' I said to myself. My uncle wouldn't sell — but my determination was bigger than his enmity.

I set up a rival shop, and thus began the extraordinary adventure that would redefine my life.

Top: Christine and I newly engaged. Bottom: On our wedding day at Paihia church, Bay of Islands, 1965.

Within seven years, we owned seven shops. After seven more years, that number had grown to 70. Now, we have more than 250 outlets across New Zealand, Australia, Canada and the United States of America, and our company is renowned as a world leader in efficient and innovative business. Having transformed both the jewellery business and the wider retail environment, we are now preparing to launch into a new chapter of our marvellous journey.

Along the way, I have spent a great deal of time reading and thinking about the path I'm on, and watching closely the experiences of the businesses around me. I've watched tycoons rise and fall, competitors enter and leave the market, staff grow and develop. I've made big mistakes, been ripped off, misjudged situations and people — and I have learned from it all. Everything that has happened, good and bad, has been part of my education. And all those lessons have distilled into a fairly simple philosophy of business and life.

It has worked for me. I believe it can work for you.

The international economy is in crisis. Businesses are failing. Unemployment is rising. Governments, not surprisingly, are alternating between practicality and panic.

But I believe the looming meltdown can be a good thing for businesses and entrepreneurs. It is possible to succeed in a downturn — in fact it is the perfect situation in which to perfect a business. Instead of fearing the side-effects of recession, wallowing in gloom and convincing ourselves the only safe haven is at home under the blankets, entrepreneurs can use this period to their advantage. With the right attitude, you can not only survive, but emerge from the crunch with a new feeling of prosperity and strength.

Here, in summary, are the ingredients of my philosophy. There are no secret herbs and spices. It is not a magic recipe — it is just a collection of solid ideas, firmly grounded in reality. All these concepts are remarkable only because they make common sense — but you'd be amazed how rarely I see them fully understood and embraced in the business world.

Don't panic

Hard times are good for you

Never be afraid of change
Hunt the right people and help them become better
Get down to the coalface
Embrace mistakes
Work is the wrong word
Keep an eye on the underdog
Visualise
Business and sentiment don't mix
Start at the bottom
Present yourself perfectly
Keep your balance
Give back and you shall receive
Find your point of difference
Money is just a yardstick

In the following chapters, I will explain each of these concepts in detail. I will tell you how my own experiences have coloured how I think about business, and share my ideas on the essential elements of a healthy organisation. With the right mental framework, you too can look forward with enthusiasm and energy to the adventure ahead.

Do not be afraid of
growing slowly, be afraid
only of standing still.
Chinese proverb

Chapter 1

DON'T
PANIC

As the global economy crunches, only one thing is certain — there will be plenty of panic.

We all know the stories about bankers flinging themselves out of skyscrapers during the Great Depression. And the last time the economy tanked quite as comprehensively, in the early 1980s, jokes about this were just the lighter side of a serious situation: fear and doomsaying were everywhere. I heard perfectly rational businesspeople predicting gloomily that their companies would inevitably collapse, that the murk would last for years, that it was the end of private enterprise as we knew it.

It was nonsense, and a complete waste of time. Certainly, the 1980s downturn was painful, as was the one that followed in the 1990s. But the entrepreneurs who survived were the ones who kept their heads in the crisis — who refused to see it as a crisis at all. They didn't sell up and scurry into corporate jobs, or retire to a backwoods cabin and take up wood-turning. They made the most of the circumstances in which we all found ourselves; using the downturn as an opportunity to tighten and trim their operations.

You can't control the international financial circumstances. All you can do is control your responses to them — and that means making the times suit you.

Of course, tightening and trimming should be part of normal business operation. Your operation should always be as lean as you can possibly make it. In a perfect world, there would be no fat to trim. But we don't operate in a perfect world. It's easy to get lazy. And that's what happens to every business, including mine, in the good times.

When business is good, our natural tendency is to relax a little. We spend our time focusing on relatively minor concerns: the shop manager who isn't performing quite as well as he or she should, the plant that is struggling to keep up with the rest of the company, the production-line process that's clunky, the client who's constantly pestering with complaints. In other words, we focus on the small flaws of our business, rather than the big strengths.

That's entirely the wrong approach. Becoming preoccupied with niggling issues is a block on the kind of broad, visionary thinking that is the real key to business success. Instead of worrying about what little things are going wrong every day, we should be thinking of the big things we are doing right — and how we can be doing them even better.

That means focusing on the shop manager who is really doing brilliantly, and paying him or her more attention.

It means seeing the parts of the production line that are performing perfectly, and noticing the staff who are keeping customers happy, from their own motivation to do well, rather than simply to be rewarded.

None of that equals ignoring the problems. On the contrary, concentrating on the good things about a business helps you see where your priorities should really lie. Once you have worked out what things are being done well, and which people are performing outstandingly, everything else will come into much clearer focus. Suddenly, you'll be able to recognise the assets within your organisation and make them even stronger.

All sorts of things will become apparent: of course you should promote Manager X, of course you should gently tell Staffer Y to change his approach to sales, of course you should rejig the production line.

Once you flip your thinking, you'll wonder why you never thought of any of this before — and that's the beauty of an economic crunch. There is nowhere to hide. There's no room for padding. A business that is flabby and sluggish will soon be exposed for what it is: sales figures will slide, profits will evaporate. If you don't perfect your business, it will begin to falter — so an economic crunch is the perfect environment for honing and finessing the way you work.

It's extraordinary the way a moment of crisis can bring things into focus — as long as you can remain calm.

My entire work life has been an illustration of this — and the ultimate example is the day that changed me for ever, the day I realised I wanted everything to change radically. Oddly enough, it was both the worst and the best day of my life.

Saturday, 1 October 1977 had started like every other day

Top: Claude Megson's design in progress, 1974.
Bottom left: Building decks with Mark and Emma.
Bottom right: Driveway construction, surrounded by native totara and kowhai.

during that time with my wife Christine and I working on our beautiful, hand-finished wooden house.

We had bought a stunning piece of land at Waikaraka, overlooking the Whangarei Harbour. The land was on top of a wooded peninsula, covered in native bush, with staggering views of the sea, and had cost us $8500. Both of us took great pride in being frugal, so we were careful to sell the house in which we'd been living before, and to pay off the debt on our pair of investment units before beginning the big job of building our dream house.

The first task was building a driveway. The Waikaraka land was incredibly steep, so we hired a local bulldozer driver to make us a zig-zagging road to the open area surrounded by native totara and kowhai trees, up to the site for our house.

We engaged the architect Claude Megson, who designed us a house of quite radical modernity — a hexagonal structure that wove its way through the totara. There were delightful little details: balconies that looked down from one level to the next, spiral staircases, a secret door that also served as a bookcase, a fire-nook that was shaped totally from concrete blocks — and upstairs, around the chimney, a folly that took you right up onto the roof.

The house had concrete block walls, lined inside and out with native tawa wood, which was my attempt at cost-cutting, after the architect had originally suggested double-brick and cedar. How naïve I was; the concrete blocks took twice as long to lay and the tawa was such a hard wood to detail that costs totally blew out. It was a good lesson for me: once you've hired an expert, you must trust them to do the job their way.

The construction was incredibly laborious; half the trucks delivering the supplies got stuck on the steep drive so we ended up buying an old tractor and trailer and driving the stuff up ourselves, and putting the concrete blocks on pallets to save the costs of a blocklayer's rate.

After nine months of work, only the first of our three levels had been built. Christine and I realised the only way to afford our dream was to scrap all the labourers and tilers and do it ourselves. Every evening after work, we would go up with the kids and place sufficient blocks on the pallets for the next

Our unusual home at Waikaraka, by architect Claude Megson, surrounded by native bush, 1976.

Christine's Mini, which she brought over from England, on Orewa Beach, 1964. It never had enough traction to get up our unsealed driveway forwards — she had to drive up every time in reverse!

day's work. We tiled all the bathrooms and kitchens ourselves, painted all the surfaces and oiled all the wood with linseed oil. I built all the hexagonal wooden decks. These were anxious, stressful times, but also great fun, with a marvellous sense of achievement. Our home was an architectural master-piece; we'd have reg-ular visits from design students keen to examine this amazing new structure.

It was not an ord-inary house, or an easy one to complete: we had constant problems with council approvals, and the driveway, which because of its grade could only be ascended by putting Christine's Mini into reverse, lost its metal every time it rained — much of the gravel got washed away in heavy rain.

We stuck with it, however, because we adored our new home so much. It was a sensational floating nightmare, perched above the Whangarei Heads, and we were besotted with it. We were going to live there for ever.

During the building, we developed a taste for possum stew — the marsupials are feral in Northland, and we'd turn the creatures we caught in our traps into delicious casseroles. It tasted a great deal like chicken — in fact, that's what most guests assumed it was, until they'd finished eating and we told them the truth. Many a visitor turned pale upon discovering what they'd just eaten.

Possum Stew

1 possum, cleaned, skinned and jointed
flour
mustard powder
dried tarragon
olive oil
onions, chopped
garlic, chopped
parsley, chopped
1 cup red wine

Dust possum joints in flour, mustard and dried tarragon.

Sear joints in skillet in olive oil. Set aside while you fry onion and garlic.

Put a layer of fried onion into a casserole dish, then possum joints, and sprinkle generously with parsley.

Make a sauce with the pan juices. Sprinkle some flour and mustard into pan, cook a few minutes, then add red wine to make a sauce. Add more wine if necessary.

Pour sauce over possum in casserole. Cook in slow oven (160°C) for at least 2 hours, maybe more, until possum is tender.

Our lives were lovely. We had two small children, Mark and Emma, and things were looking good professionally, too: I was still working at my uncle's jewellery shop, Fishers, but I had won a competition for window displays run by the Bulova watch company of Switzerland, and they flew Christine and me to Switzerland, where we met all the company's top executives.

But I wasn't entirely happy. I had a constant awareness that there must be more to life than working in my uncle's store. At least, I wanted there to be more. I had begun reading motivational books, such as the works of Dennis Waitley, Earl Nightingale and Dale Carnegie, and I'd formed the goal of opening my own jewellery shop.

Thanks to the expert staff-training and management of my late father Dickie, who had worked at Fishers for decades, it was a thriving little business; we took great pride in the fact we never let anyone leave the shop without something sparkling on some part of their body.

Working together at the shop, Christine and I had also investigated clever marketing concepts, such as holding special events and theme nights to entice a new breed of customer through the door. One was a Japanese night to promote our pearls; we hired a Japanese lady in a kimono to host our guests, Christine festooned the store with pink blossom branches made from crêpe paper, and we displayed giant hanks of pearls around the shop. We handed out cans of oysters with every purchase, and in every 50th can was a pearl necklace — a gimmick that got the town talking.

But despite all our innovations and passion, my uncle Arthur still owned the shop. Arthur was slowly retiring from daily involvement, but he installed an accountant, who had inherited Arthur's misgivings about me.

This accountant didn't approve of me one bit, and was sceptical and suspicious every time I tried to suggest something new. Eventually, I decided I'd had enough. In 1971 Christine and I heard of a jewellery store for sale in Taupo, in the central North Island, and we drove down to check it out — but on our return, Arthur was waiting.

'You can't do this, son,' he said.

Arthur gave me a pay rise, and I agreed to stay.

I still wonder why. Deep down, I knew I wanted to go. I knew I could do better than managing my uncle's store. And I couldn't really blame Arthur for offering more money; he was just trying to hang on to his store manager.

The truth was that I was afraid to leave. I was terrified of leaving my comfort zone, or making a mistake. And life was easy in Whangarei; the whole town knew who I was and my customers were people who would just drop in for a chat on their way past. I knew them as much as they knew me. If we went to Taupo, I knew I could set up the shop but I wasn't so sure I could attract customers. And we both liked Whangarei.

It was so easy to come up with excuses, so we stopped talking about moving on or owning our own shop. I convinced myself I was making the right decision by staying in Whangarei.

It didn't earn me the respect of the accountant, either. One day, hunched over the calculator in the back room at Fishers, he was tutting and harrumphing about the cost of my promotional activities and my increased wage.

'You might have champagne tastes but you'll always be on a beer income,' he told me. 'You'd better cut your cloth to suit your income and not expect another raise.'

The conversation depressed me enormously. But I found a great release in our house-building project. It was my own time, when I didn't have to think about my work frustrations, and could focus on Christine and the family.

After a long day of working on finishing off the house that spring Saturday in 1977, I suggested a movie. Afterwards we drove to Christine's parents' house, where Mark and Emma were to spend the evening while we went to a dinner

As I watched my home dissolve into a pile of burnt stumps and ashes, I realised that everything had to change. 'I'm going to buy my uncle's business,' I said aloud, standing there amid the damp wreckage.

party. As we stood around chatting with Christine's parents, the phone rang. 'I don't know how to tell you this,' said our neighbour, Mrs Strongman, 'but your house is on fire.'

At first, Christine thought it was a joke, and laughed — but Mrs Strongman was serious. My first reaction was panic; I knew the house was under-insured, and the contents weren't insured at all. I had been meaning to sort out the details but — isn't it always the way — I hadn't got around to it.

We jumped in the car and hurtled towards home. I can't remember a second of the journey, except the moment we rounded the corner on Whangarei Heads Road. Across the bay, there was our house, nestled in the bush. Bright orange flames rose at least 20 metres into the sky. It was raining heavily, but the rain was not doing anything to dampen the flames. The house was an inferno. Christine burst into tears, but I became eerily calm as we raced along the road. It's all over, I thought.

When we finally reached the house, there were people rushing and clambering everywhere; firemen racing up and down the drive with ladders and hoses. One of the fire engines was stuck on our driveway — the tight corners were too sharp for the cumbersome truck to negotiate. I had half-emptied our swimming pool, but the firemen were pumping out the remaining water and spraying it at the base of the flames. None of it made a bit of difference. Our dream house was gone.

We stood as close as we could get. We were in shock, and as we gazed at the fire, strange thoughts occurred to us.

'Oh, there's my shirt on the clothesline,' Christine pointed out. 'I should go down and grab it.' At that moment, one entire side of the house exploded. Perhaps best not to rescue the laundry, then.

Christine wanted me to save her jewellery from our bedroom, which was in a part of the house still untouched by the flames. (I must point out here, for the sake of matrimonial harmony, that Christine claims she actually suggested retrieving my prized violin, and that her jewellery just happened to be nearby.) Anyway, I bolted into the house, snatching what little treasure I could get my hands on. The atmosphere inside was choking, and I could barely see what I was doing. The left wing of the house was separated from the rest by a central fire-nook with insulated brick walls, and the flames were all on the other side — but the heat coming through the walls was extraordinarily intense. As I sprinted down the stairs to escape, the curtains on the other side of the room burst into flames, such was the heat coming through the wall. Indeed, the radiant heat was so intense that a couple of gold pocket-watches on the mantelpiece melted into globules.

After my foolhardy rescue mission, in which I had managed to salvage both the violin and some of Christine's jewellery, we scrambled to the top of the hill and watched the house burn.

We'll never know what caused the fire. We had been putting linseed and turpentine on the walls, and there was a suggestion at the time that this concoction sometimes combusts. Another theory the fire brigade and our neighbours put forth was that we'd left the television on and it overheated. The idea of arson did cross our minds, but the fire officers thought that unlikely.

In a strange way, I don't really care what caused the blaze.

People who have near-death experiences often say their lives flash before their eyes. Something similar happened to me. As we watched the fire, my mind was raging with everything I had — and had not — done with my life. I could vividly see moments of my life appearing in my mind, and all the things I had once vaguely hoped my life might be.

And it occurred to me, very simply and clearly, as I watched my home dissolve into a pile of burnt stumps and ashes, that everything must change.

'I'm going to buy my uncle's business,' I said aloud, standing there amid the damp wreckage.

Exactly what happened next will unfold in the chapters to come. But here's the message: the worst imaginable disaster, the destruction of the house I loved so much, was to be the best thing that ever happened to me. It forced me into a calm resolve, a determination to change everything completely. It taught me the value of keeping one's head in a time of trauma — and the transformative power of hardship. And for all of that, I will be eternally grateful.

After the fire

The night our house burned down, we had been invited to a dinner party. Once the flames were extinguished, we thought we might as well go along anyway.

We were a little late, of course, and our hosts Chris Busck and his wife Martine were getting worried about us. Chris had rung our home number several times, and had convinced himself I was being held hostage by robbers who wanted the keys to the Fishers safe. As we drove slowly towards the Buscks' house, we encountered Chris coming the other way — he was heading to our house with a shotgun.

It was the most emotional dinner party imaginable. With the Buscks and our mutual friends Clive and Neen Williams, we ate (rabbit, I think, although it could have been possum) and drank and laughed and cried.

Christine now often says she believes that night helped us heal from the trauma of the fire. We didn't go straight to bed, feeling sorry for ourselves and picking through the rubble of our lives. We just had fun.

There certainly wasn't any fun to be had the next day. Christine felt it was important to show Mark and Emma what had happened, so we returned to the house with them, and together we picked through the soggy debris.

It was miserable.

Poor Emma, who was only six, was beside herself because her favourite toy, Mother Pig, was gone. Christine had made Mother Pig herself out of red velvet, with press-studs on her belly. Inside were six little piglets, each with a press-stud on its nose, so it could be snapped onto its mother's belly to be suckled. Emma loved Mother Pig, and sobbed when she couldn't find her. The next week, Christine went into town to buy a sewing machine and fabric — and by the time Emma came home from school, a new Mother Pig was ready and waiting. She is still one of Emma's cherished possessions.

The loss of cuddly toys is one of the unexpected hardships of a fire. Mark was terribly sad at the loss of all his own little friends, and although friends and neighbours — and complete strangers — were incredibly generous in giving us clothes and gifts, Mark didn't get any soft toys. He got plenty of other toys and gadgets, but as an eight year old, he was considered too old for teddy-bears, I guess. Christine fixed that too: she got out the sewing machine and made Mark a large frog, filled with little tadpoles. He loved the frog, and still has her, too.

The effects on Christine and I were profound and emotional. I couldn't pass the driveway without shaking and for quite a long time afterwards, a big red wall of flames would appear in front of me. It was quite odd. I suppose it was post-traumatic stress of some kind or another; not surprising when you consider the drama of losing everything we had in a few moments.

When the insurance assessors came, they had a look around and said they would pay out $120,000 for the loss of the house — a sizeable sum in 1977, but not the total value of the property, by any means.

As for the contents, it was tough luck: we hadn't insured them.

As we salvaged and mended and worried about the practicalities of life, my dramatic decision about my future was still bubbling away in my subconscious.

On the Monday after the fire, Christine and I both returned to work. I was confronted with the accountant, who was as unfriendly and cold as usual. I got on with my day, thinking to myself: I'm going to buy this business.

For Christine, the first day back at work was awful. She was teaching part-time at Kamo High School, and one of her pupils came in late.

'You're late,' Christine said to him.

'And your house burnt down,' he snarled.

Christine was horrified at his rudeness. She left the class, went straight to the headmaster, handed in her resignation and left, never to return again.

It turned out to be a wonderful liberation for Christine. Relieved of the stress of teaching and the responsibility of caring for

From Christine's puriri tree exhibition.

the house, she suddenly had more time for the children, and for her first love: art.

She produced a series of drawings and ink paintings of the gnarled trunks of New Zealand native puriri trees, which we displayed in an exhibition in a little showroom at the Fishers store. On our opening night, we sold the whole show — a thrill for Christine and, I felt, a new beginning for us.

We rented a semi-finished house near the Whangarei Harbour. As we dealt with our devastated architect and the business of buying all the necessary items of a household, we couldn't bear to visit the site of our ruined home. But after a few months in rented houses we began searching for another block of land on which to build.

Christine's father Frank rang us one day with a piece of sound advice: 'Consider what you already have. That land is stunning. You have poured too much into this property to just walk away.'

Frank was right, and we decided to rebuild on the same site, engaging a builder and hiring the local football team, who were raising funds, to clean out the shell of our home and help us repaint the remaining walls and reconstruct the rest. The house was never the same grandiose structure, but we were busy and happy with our project, and moved back in after one year.

We were paranoid about the safety of our newly rebuilt home. We had a master power switch installed by the front door, so we could cut off all power as we left. I've been a big fan of smoke alarms ever since, and even today before I leave a house, I always go around and close all internal doors. Our fire taught me about the power of a draught, which can suck the flames through open doorways and accelerate the blaze.

Our sense of fragile security was heightened by a robbery at our house soon after we'd moved back in. Jewellery, antique pieces and a large bottle of Chanel perfume were all taken — so we installed a burglar alarm and bought a big Doberman, which we named Phoenix.

Christine and Phoenix, 1981.

A few weeks later, Christine and the children were home one night while I worked late. She heard a car revving around the corners of the drive, so she called the children and Phoenix to the front deck above the driveway. A really menacing man opened the door of the car, got out and saw them on the balcony.

'Wrong house,' he said, getting back into the car.

We were so far out of town that by the time police arrived, it was all too late — but we still believe this was one of our robbers.

The fire taught us to appreciate our great fortune in having a healthy, united, happy family. It showed us the value of security and smoke alarms. And it entirely changed my outlook on life: I was now determined to buy my uncle's business.

The only question was, Where was I going to get the money?

I needed to find someone to back me and, not for the first time in my life, my violin came to the rescue. As an adult, I had continued my childhood love of music, often playing in either a trio or a quartet with friends like Evie Knight, who played the cello and piano, and her husband Nigel, who played the violin and viola. Nigel was a wealthy man, having inherited a great deal of money, and he was the first person I thought of approaching to be my financial partner.

'Would you go in to help me buy my uncle's business?' I asked Nigel.

To my astonishment, he was thrilled to be involved — and even better, he would put in as much money I needed, asking for only a 20 per cent stake in the business in return.

The only catch was persuading my uncle to sell.

I told my parents Billie and Dickie about my plan, and they were supportive. Through their five per cent shareholding in Fishers, we were able to get access to the books, to make an assessment of the business's worth. I hadn't a clue how to value a business, so local accountant Wally Yovich came up with a figure for me and I put it to the accountant, to be taken to Arthur.

He rejected the offer.

I wasn't going to be dissuaded. Nigel and I put in another offer for a sum much greater than what the business was worth — and this time even the accountant was impressed.

'I'll take the offer to Arthur,' he said with something approximating approval, a most unfamiliar mood in our dealings, 'but it'll take three weeks to give you an answer.'

I thought we had it. What retired jeweller wouldn't sell his business, at top dollar, to the nephew who had worked in it for 23 years — the only son of his only, younger sister, who had worked there herself, and whose husband had worked there as well?

However, I began making discreet enquiries about other options, just in case the impossible happened and Arthur refused to sell. I found a bustling, lively little grocery store near the corner of Cameron and Rathbone streets just down from Fishers, which I thought would make a great location for a jewellery shop. I approached the owner and asked if he'd ever be interested in moving, and he did not seem terribly keen. After a few weeks of thinking about it, the grocer gave me a call: he'd had a change of heart, and was now keen to move.

'I've found other premises,' he said, 'but I need to know now if you want the shop or not.'

The timing was terrible. We were still waiting for word from Arthur. What if we ended up with two shops, when it had taken me all this time to decide I even wanted one? I asked Nigel for advice, and he told me to take the grocery shop, just in case. We would sort out the problem later, he said.

It was a good call.

'Well, I'm surprised at your uncle,' the accountant eventually told me, 'but he's decided not to sell to you at any price.'

I was astonished and appalled. He asked what I planned to do, and I said I'd leased alternative premises and was preparing to set up in competition to Fishers. We sat there, not speaking. There didn't seem to be anything to say.

'Look,' I eventually told him, 'I've been here for 23 years, so I'll stay for two or three months to help get a manager up and running for you before I leave.'

He looked at his watch. It was about 10.45 in the morning.

'If you make it sharp,' he said, 'you can be out of here by eleven.'

All in the family

Family businesses can be tricky places to work. Fishers had been founded by my maternal grandfather, Herman Bruno Fritsche. Herman was a bit of a mystery — we never quite knew where in Switzerland he came from before he migrated to New Zealand in the early 1900s. All we knew was that he was a gifted clockmaker, a trade that had been passed down through many generations in the Fritsche family. Family legend held that he had made watches for the Russian aristocracy, but when he arrived in Auckland with his English wife Emily, he also proved a talented businessman, running a thriving jewellery shop on Karangahape Road, at the southern end of Queen Street, and living in a huge house in St Stephen's Avenue, Parnell with their six children, the youngest of whom was my mother.

They had a ballroom and servants and, at its peak, the jewellery shop employed 25 full-time watchmakers. Herman anglicised his name to Fisher and embraced his good fortune.

The Fisher family at Waimate North, circa 1920. My mother Billie is front left, next to her mum.

Then came the Depression and the poor man lost everything. That's how the family came to Whangarei. After a brief and unsuccessful attempt at dairy farming, Grandfather started another jewellery shop — and by the time my father Dickie

The original Fishers Jewellers store, started by my grandfather and run by Uncle Arthur.

arrived on the scene, Uncle Arthur was firmly in charge.

Both my parents worked for a wage in the shop, a situation that suited Dickie quite well — but it really riled my mother. She thought she should have been given a share of the business, but Uncle Arthur was not inclined to relinquish control. He didn't seem to feel too fond of my father or me.

Dickie put up with it; he was a talented engraver and jeweller, but his real gift was for sales. He devoted himself to becoming the best salesman anyone could imagine, using all his natural talents of kindness, charm and persuasion to make a great deal of money for Uncle Arthur.

For all her frustration, Billie never did anything about the situation. She never confronted Arthur — she simply wasn't a confrontational type of woman — and it was an era when it seemed entirely natural for a business to pass through the men in a family, without much consideration for women's claims.

For my whole childhood, Billie and Dickie worked side by side in the shop, smiling at the customers as if everything was wonderful.

Never give in.
Never, never, never, never.
Sir Winston Churchill

Chapter 2

TOUGH TIMES ARE GOOD FOR YOU

I don't believe I've ever had bad luck in my life. An ill wind has never blown me away. I've had plenty of difficult times — but I firmly believe every hardship has helped me. That might sound like an easy thing to say for a businessman of my age — but my career is nowhere near finished. I'm still building my business, and every day I wake up thinking about ways to develop our brand, advance our prospects and — most importantly — to keep enjoying life and the challenge.

It's a truism of our times that the generation of people who lived through the Great Depression are resourceful, thoughtful, frugal people — they know what it's like to make do with very little money, and they have a level of understanding about the importance of hard work that subsequent generations have often lacked.

We're all used to hearing someone say that a difficult period or a crunch in our lives is character-building. That can be a very irritating phrase — but as annoying as it can be when we're mired in a stressful situation, the sentiment is entirely true. What doesn't kill us certainly does make us stronger. For individuals, that principle is played out whenever there's a personal hardship to overcome. I'm the perfect example. Our business would never have existed at all without the 'disaster' of the house fire. I simply would never have had the impetus to give myself a kick that could have compared with that fire: it was so huge and dramatic and violent that I had no excuse but to act on making my dreams into reality.

So, at a personal level, challenges are great for us: but I believe they are also good for business.

One of the big problems in business life is staying fresh, particularly if you are lucky enough to be a leader in your field, or if you don't have a direct competitor breathing down your neck. In those circumstances, an external prod is often what is necessary.

And a great big one has just come our way: yours, mine and everyone else in business around the world. The current global economic crisis is the perfect time to become really focused on your business. It is a chance to think about what you're doing well, and what you're not. It might, depending upon your field, be a perfect time to shrink your staff numbers or recalibrate your business systems to cut costs in some other way: Can you move a processing plant to another location? Should your delivery systems be reassessed? Does every regional office or suburban outlet need a thorough analysis to assess how things could be done better?

Of course, you can do all these things at any time, in any business; in fact, you should be thinking these things all the time. So why don't we? Because it's all a bit too hard, and in times of easy fortune, there's very little incentive.

The difference in a time of economic downturn is that you become amazingly clear-headed about it all. You can't romanticise a business when profits are shrinking and cashflow is tight, or talk yourself into thinking that it's okay to run an inefficient process because there are more important things to worry about than whether every widget is being sourced at the lowest cost, or how much time is being wasted in team meetings. The truth is that those little things are vital to making a business work well — and right now, there is no excuse to ignore them.

In the case of Michael Hill International, the crisis has forced us to soul-search. I've been in business for more than five decades, and I've had great fortune along the way. My company has risen to the top and that can be a problem: I believe there's a real risk that prosperity can make our business, like any other company, flabby and lazy.

As in all businesses, we've often caught ourselves tolerating things we really shouldn't: staff who aren't quite at the top of their game; shops that might not be making the level of profit they should; structures that don't quite work perfectly. Now is the perfect time to iron out all of that: and so we're taking the opportunity to reshape our business, with an eye to the future.

Let me run through the principles underpinning this reassessment. They're ideas that I think should lie at the foundation of any realistic recalibration of a business, now more than ever.

What are we doing well? That's easy. We have created a brilliant business where nothing existed before: jewellery for the mid-market customer who values quality at an affordable price. We've associated our name — my name — with the values of reliability, innovation, quality and excellent service.

What could we do better? In some of our markets — especially Australia and New Zealand — we have earned a reputation as a discounter, offering bargains no other retailer could match. That perception is of our own creation, and it worked brilliantly for us when we were building the brand. But now that we have become so large, we have gradually come to realise we had been doing certain things that required a lot of energy without yielding us as much return as they could: for example, reselling brand-name watches. We used to sell a great many other-brand-name watches, making a small margin on each watch. That's a perfectly good business model, and it worked well for us for many years, but we soon came to recognise that there was a great deal of untapped potential in each transaction. We began to think: What if we created our own watch brand? What if instead of buying a Rado, Seiko or Casio, people bought a Michael Hill? That way we could simultaneously increase our profit margin and build our brand into something else. Why not extend our reputation into an exciting new area?

What sort of business could we become? A luxury brand of our own? It's always dangerous to compare oneself with other labels, but we realised there was no reason why we couldn't achieve some of the name recognition and cachet of, for example, Hugo Boss. The key here would be not extending ourselves too far: we wouldn't want to get into areas we knew nothing about, like clothes or shoes (an area where we had one disastrous foray in the past, which I'll tell you about later). But there are certain items that naturally belong in a jewellery shop, and that complement the rest of our stock: for example, pens or fragrances.

At the basis of all our considerations is one really important lesson we've learned over the years. Winston Churchill summed it up best: only fight on one front at once. It's very dangerous to engage in several battles at once, to decide a whole business needs overhauling, and begin attacking it from all angles.

So as you are going through the process of reassessing and honing your business, be careful not to take on too many fights at the same time. Look at things in an overall, holistic sense and then isolate the areas you can improve one by one. By perfecting one element of the business at a time, you're never in danger of overexposing yourself to risk.

Here's an example of streamlining that really worked for us. Funnily enough, it wasn't economic crisis that brought it about, but another kind of disaster: personality clash.

In the late 1980s and for most of 1990, there was a growing feeling of unrest in the company. At the time, we were very strong in New Zealand and on the way to becoming equally robust in Australia. Christine and I were living in Brisbane, Mike Parsell was running the fledgling Australian side of the business, and Howard Bretherton was running New Zealand, which was doing very well. But there seemed to be a lot of pressure on us to do better in Australia — rivalry that came from within our own ranks.

We had attempted to move into retailing shoes, which hadn't worked, and it soon became clear that animosity over the failed experiment was splitting the company into two camps.

Howard worked the New Zealand arm of the business hard and really wrung the most out of it. Over in Brisbane, Mike and I thought he was doing brilliantly, but what we didn't realise was that Howard felt left out: Mike and I had been working together for three years, sharing everything and spending a great deal of time together, from the walk downtown to the shop floor, where we would sell together, to the buying trips we made together and our joint meetings about hiring staff.

Without our really noticing, two different companies had developed. Our Australian and New Zealand arms had different computer systems, different shop designers and builders, separate accounts, and even different jewellery buyers, who had each developed separate deals from the same supplier.

Of course, sometimes the rivalry was a good thing: it created competition between Mike and Howard to have the top-performing business. But it simply wasn't sustainable. If we were to become a global brand, we simply couldn't have this kind of duplication and competition in two rival head offices; it was unnecessarily expensive and confusing for staff and suppliers. We needed to reshape the business, but Howard wasn't interested in changing things. He said he wanted things to stay just as they were — and because I found that unacceptable, Howard decided to leave. It was a great shame to lose Howard's experience and creativity, but it was time for us to change.

Mike was immediately made chief executive officer of Michael Hill Jeweller, and I shared with him a vision I'd been developing for several months: I had visualised us moving from a New Zealand-Australian company to a global player with 1000 stores within 20 years — a major step!

First conference at our Waikaraka home, 1980. From left: Nigel Knight, Howard Bretherton, Mike Parsell, Henry Cunningham, Andy Rout and Hamish Sharma. Front: Me and Nigel Keith.

'Let me think about it,' Mike said when I raised the idea with him.

Mike was never one for quick decisions. Some weeks later, he came to me and said he'd had enough time to think about my idea.

'It's achievable,' he said. 'We can do it.'

I was thrilled.

We all knew that if we were to be a worldwide company, we couldn't have more than one head office. We decided to close the Whangarei headquarters. Why Whangarei and not Brisbane? Well, because Whangarei was at the end of the line it was hard to get stock in and out because of the lack of an international airport. We needed to have our headquarters in a city that was truly connected to the rest of the world, because in a global structure, we needed our distribution centre, manufacturing site and hub for meetings to be easily accessible for the rest of the world.

The move made our business much stronger.

The truth was that tension had created the solution: we'd been forced to identify the source of the problem within the company, and move past it. And now we had the beginnings of an exciting new era: the truly international future of our company.

Best of all, we had a common goal, and a united feeling among our team. As soon as the word spread among our staff that we were aiming for 1000 stores in 20 years, the attitude of the whole team changed. Everyone, from the shop floor to the boardroom, could get excited about the future: promotions, adventures and exploring new territory.

It wasn't easy for everyone — morale crashed in New Zealand when we closed the local head office, and many of our people didn't cope well with the idea of change, because they saw themselves as potentially losing out.

But here again, this was a case of an issue that challenged, worried and then strengthened us. Some of our New Zealand managers — the ones who just couldn't cope with the changing nature of the business — left the company, and in their place we engaged people who were excited and positive about the future.

With only one head office, and an energised workforce, we had a far more profitable business, which was quicker on its feet and simpler to run: and that made everything leaner. It took a bit of pain to get there, but without the pain, we wouldn't have got the payoff — and that was the lesson.

Michael Hill staff story: Leah James
Store manager, New Plymouth

If someone had said to me 10 years ago that Michael Hill would ask me to write about myself in his book, my answer would have been the same as every other New Zealander I know: Yeah, right!

I went off to my interview for my first Michael Hill job wearing a borrowed outfit and $70 acrylic nails. I was 10-foot-tall and bulletproof until I was asked: 'What's your five-year plan?'

GULP! What five-year plan? Hell, my only plan was getting through the interview, picking up the boys after school and thinking about what we would have for dinner that night! Thinking quickly, I said something to do with the Greek islands.

I started as a sales professional in the Nelson store in August 1998 and shortly afterwards I became assistant manager. By Christmas 2001, I was offered a position at the New Plymouth store, which allowed me to move my family back home to Taranaki. I had a fabulous team and turnover grew steadily, blitzing all targets out of the water.

I put my hand up for expansion into Canada in September 2002. I was the only Kiwi to be employed as a manager, and off I went. Who would have thought that me, Leah James, married and a mother at 17, would be helping to open a New Zealand icon in a foreign country. It was not quite the Greek islands — but close enough.

Since Canada I have been able to go into stores and support managers and work alongside the many talented staff that Michael Hill carefully selects to make our teams so powerful. It takes a lot of hard work, sweat and tears to achieve the awards that only the elite selling teams win — many of which, I can proudly boast, my team has!

Michael Hill staff story: Althena Birch
Store manager, Whangarei

Before Michael Hill Jeweller, I was a concrete worker, trying to keep up with the boys. I made paving slabs, water troughs and even tried my hand at plastering a few water tanks — all this with a baby in tow, and I mean that literally. He was quite often sleeping next to me in a wheelbarrow.

Who would have thought that someone like me — a mother

of two at the age of 19, with no education other than life itself — could become someone people aspire to be like?

I had nothing but a love of sparkling things and a desire to make something of myself the day I walked into the Michael Hill store in Whangarei.

I started at the bottom, learning the art and the science of selling emotion-based products. I began to realise that this was more than just a job, it was a vehicle to life.

The Michael Hill way of business taught me that people are the true key. Trust me when I say times weren't always rosy, but tell me what job that deals with people is?

After finding success as a sales professional, I was encouraged to be a leader and manager of people and systems. To do this I had to make a sacrifice — one that at the time wrenched my world apart. Little did I know it would make me one of Michael's best managers.

I moved to Wellington to run a $2.6 million store, leaving behind my wonderful husband and two children in Whangarei. I only saw them twice in seven months and ran up a big phone bill. Twelve months later I was back home in Whangarei. Two years after that the Whangarei store was a $3 million business.

In today's trade, people say things are tough and maybe they are. The world is a harder place and if there's one thing this business has taught me it is to remember the little things: like believing in people, and having standards and systems and using and sticking to them. Daring to dream and having goals is not a sin. Write them down and look at them. If you lose your way, go back to the basics, as they will never fail you: the truth is in the results.

The biggest lesson I've learned is that I will only ever be as good as the people that work for me, along side me and with me.

Dare to believe and dream.

Michael Hill staff story: Lynn Alexander
Retired store manager

I immigrated to Australia in 1993, where I worked in jewellery sales for the first time. I started with Michael Hill in 1994. Early in 1995, the Michael Hill Training System was introduced. It was welcomed by most, as we now had targets and goals to set and achieve. The top goal was the Gold Club. So I set my sights on being in the first Gold Club and was one of only 19 to achieve this in Australia, and did so for the following three years until I became the third-top sales person in the company. I then became a store manager, increasing both the sales and net profit.

My next challenge, at another store, was to find, hire and train a new team. Within six months the team was complete and meeting all targets. Then I was dealt a blow — I was diagnosed with breast cancer. Within one week I had a lumpectomy and began chemotherapy, and then radiation. To take my mind off what the drugs were doing to me, I focused on my team and the daily running of the store. There were good days and bad ones, but we all came out the other side stronger and more positive.

Next I was sent to a Brisbane store. It was a $1.7 million store, but capable of $2 million. The first year I again had to find, hire and train a new team. We almost got there, with $1.9 million, and the following year we were just short of $2 million.

My age has never been an issue for me or Michael Hill. When I reached 60, my husband was diagnosed with cancer, and I decided to step down from management and go back to sales. I set myself a challenge to reach the Platinum Club and I achieved this for both 2007 ($275K of sales) and 2008 ($500K of sales).

A few things in particular have helped me be successful over the years: my toughest critic is myself; I have the highest personal and professional standards; I believe in myself and the others around me; I believe everyone is unique and I treat others with the respect they deserve.

A fanatic is one who can't
change his mind and won't
change the subject.
Sir Winston Churchill

Chapter 3

NEVER BE AFRAID OF CHANGE

I used to spend a great deal of my life being terrified. I worried about what people thought of me. I fretted over the frustrations of my unfulfilled ambitions. And most of all, I feared the changes I knew my life needed.

But once I began transforming my life, I realised there was nothing to fear. Change, which once had been so frightening, became the greatest thrill imaginable. And now I can't get enough; I'm a little addicted to change. If the business stays the same for too long, I'm concerned we aren't reactive enough, or that it's time to shake things up. I'm not talking about needless upheaval, but the constant, invigorating revolution that keeps us all alive.

In the past three decades, we have dramatically altered

our business several times: by venturing into new territories, rethinking our approach to issues and constantly devising ways to alter our old habits. 'If it ain't broke, don't fix it' is a cute maxim, but it doesn't apply to all businesses in all situations. The reality is if it ain't broke, keep looking at it to see if you can fix it anyway.

The fire was a painful jolt, one I wouldn't wish on my worst enemy. But it was the shock that clarified exactly what I wanted. One of the reasons I am writing this book is to encourage others to take the leap — hopefully without anything as traumatic as having a Mother Pig go up in a roaring blaze to prompt you into action.

I don't think all jolts need to be so dramatic. I think a jolt could be as simple as picking up this book and realising that now is the time to start acting on the dreams you've always had.

Humans are naturally comfortable, complacent creatures. We like being cosy. If we don't get the occasional prod from a red-hot poker of some description, we're liable to spend our lives sitting snugly on our sofas, waiting for good things to happen to us.

That was definitely my trouble before the fire. I certainly had the ability to change. I knew what I wanted out of life. I had read all the books, listened to all the tapes — like Dale Carnegie, I wanted to win friends and influence people.

But change, for me, was just too hard. I couldn't be bothered.

Complacency is the enemy of progress. Without the odd jolt, there's no need for us to try a little bit harder, or put a little extra spirit into our tasks.

It's great to form long-term goals. Ambitions and dreams are what keep us getting up in the mornings. But whatever your goal is, it needs action now. I wanted my uncle's business — and once my complacency had been burnt to a pile of smouldering bricks, I could see that clearly. And finally, at the age of 40, I had the guts to make my move.

On the night of the fire, when we arrived at our dinner party, I made a note to myself on the back of a business card. 'Buy my uncle's business,' the note said. Those four words put me ahead: at last, my goal was clear in my mind, and because it was tangible, written down in front of me, I had to take it seriously.

I wish, often, that I had never been so afraid of change. I don't think I knew I was living in fear, but that was the reality. I was too timid, too terrified, to effect the change I knew my life needed.

But once I started, there was no looking back.

Three weeks after they showed me the door at Fishers, Christine and I opened our first Michael Hill shop in Whangarei. Those three weeks had passed in a blur — a wonderful, exciting, invigorating blur.

The day I left Fishers, two of the best staff quit to follow me. By Easter three more had also defected. It was a great advantage for a start-up business: I already had a full staff, trained and ready to go.

We went boating with friends over Easter and dreamt

Fishers the Jewellers, circa 1950.

up logos and storefronts, fantasising about gleaming jewels. We decided we'd simply call the shop Michael Hill Jeweller, trading on the fact that most people in town already knew who I was. We were so excited that we could barely wait to begin. Christine drew the Michael Hill logo on some graph paper while we were at sea, and outside a pub in the Bay of Islands, I got chatting to a lady we knew and sold her a diamond ring from my soon-to-be-opened shop.

Christine had a clear vision for the store's layout, and employed a draughtsman and builder. She took much inspiration from Hong Kong, where we had been to the gold markets and seen the wide open shopfronts with entire families gathered behind the U-shaped counters, just waiting to sell their wares.

We had a Hong Kong-style U-shaped counter and small windows, just as we'd seen in Switzerland, and a roller door. The fashion at the time was for a tiny doorway with massive

We had just opened the first store — myself, Christine, Mark and Emma, 1979.

windows, but we thought the opposite approach would be a good way to usher customers through the doors — they would pause to look in the little windows, with their clever displays, and before they knew it, they would be stepping inside.

Simplicity was to be our hallmark. Fishers had sold countless lines of stock, but we wanted to specialise in jewellery only.

Our shop was tiny, and so was our clout: we were up against one of the most well-known and prosperous businesses in the country and, not surprisingly, many of the people we dealt with were nervous about offending or alienating Fishers. Our chosen insurance company, for example, declined to insure us because they also insured Fishers, and felt there was a conflict of interest — the same argument I got from several suppliers, who were nervous about losing the Fishers account.

Our very first full-page newspaper advert — May 1979. It was drastically different to anything else published around that time.

None of this bothered us. Part of our approach, right from the beginning, was to view every obstacle as a challenge to be overcome. Because we didn't have insurance before our opening, I found myself spending the night in the shop on the eve of our debut, to fend off would-be robbers. With every inconvenience I just got more excited. Nothing was going to stop me.

We opened on a Sunday, 13 May 1979, putting trestle tables out on the street and serving wine and cheese to the crowds of invited guests who flocked along. It was a lovely festival atmosphere, prompted by the fact our store was far too small to cope with a sizeable crush. We poured a glass of champagne for everyone who arrived, and people wandered in and out of the shop, chatting and laughing and — wonders — buying jewellery.

I don't think anyone other than Christine and I really thought that our own jewellery shop would take off. I remember Tim Sullivan from a nearby menswear store preparing me for the days when there would be no customers and no money in the till.

'Those days hurt,' he said kindly.

We never had one — and here is my theory on why. We were different. We were fresh and innovative — and that made us exciting and attractive to our customers.

We looked modern, our stock was different (partly because we had to use different suppliers) and we were full of unusual marketing ideas. I bought acres of space in the local newspaper and time on the local radio station, where we ran interviews with people in the street, talking about this chap Michael Hill and the jewellery he was selling.

With Nigel Knight in the back room doing the books, I was firmly on the shop floor, and never left. That was part

Christine drawing illustrations for our early catalogues.

of Dickie's training — a good salesman knows exactly what is happening on his sales floor. Just like my father, I was always there to help a sale along, greet a customer, or help my team work out where things were going wrong on the rare occasions when a customer failed to buy anything.

Christine drew illustrations of our jewellery for the newspaper ads and dressed the windows, changing the displays every Monday and installing inventive props, which drew a regular crowd of shoppers, curious to see what would be next. One window was a particular crowd-stopper: Christine's father had made a mesh cage, sprayed it gold and filled it with six-day-old chicks. The jewellery was displayed on top of the cage.

Part of what defined us was what we didn't have: there were no trophy cups, no cuckoo clocks, no Lladro or Dresden, no silverware, nothing to distract the customer from our core business of diamond rings and jewellery.

The store was always vibrant, buzzing with music and chatter. We trained our salespeople to get chatting to the customers about anything other than jewellery: the weather, the customers' clothing, the latest rugby score. The message was: you're welcome here. No pressure. We're pleased to see you. At some point, the salesperson would politely discover what the customer was looking for. Invariably, a sale would follow — the customers were relaxed and happy, the salespeople were confident and welcoming, and the cash register was ringing.

In our first nine months, we turned over $225,000. By the second year it was $750,000, putting us right up there with the top jewellery shops in the country — including the old family business.

In our third year, we cracked $1 million.

Christine and I loved our new lives. We never stopped for a moment to doubt the future, leaping out of bed each morning to rush to work, and delighting in the financial success it was bringing us — and it was all happening because I had finally got over my fear.

As soon as the Whangarei shop was running smoothly, we began looking around for a second outlet. Why not? Now that I had made my first big step, I had learned a lesson that would shape the rest of my life: change is nothing to be afraid of. Indeed, it is the essence of success.

At a broader strategic level,

Michael Hill Jeweller

CHRISTMAS CATALOGUE 1981

$265
$448
$265

$250
$436
$250

$40 BEACH UMBRELLA
FREE
WITH ANY DIAMOND RING
PURCHASED BY DECEMBER 12

Michael Hill Jeweller

180 HIGH STREET, LOWER HUTT
255W HERETAUNGA STREET, HASTINGS
24 CAMERON STREET, WHANGAREI

Drawings by Christine on the front page of the 1981 catalogue.

change has always invigorated us, and our business. When we moved into Australia, and later when we shifted to Canada, we had to reframe and hone the business from the foundations to the top.

In 2008 Michael Hill Jeweller made a move into the US. We had done all the research, but you have to test the water, so we purchased 17 jewellery stores which were part of the Whitehall Jewellery chain, with many stores across the US. Whitehall had gone into receivership, and it was a golden opportunity to secure these sites, located in prime positions in shopping centres in greater Chicago and St Louis. It was an amazing deal to get the sites and stock at 80 cents in the dollar, including fitouts and positions.

In hindsight, the timing may not have been perfect, as the recession in the US has become worse than we initially envisaged. But if it wasn't for the downturn, it would have been impossible to secure such prime locations.

We now have the opportunity to fully understand and work in the market that has the greatest potential for us in the future.

Tough times produce the best opportunities to expand your horizons. Every time, we've emerged from the process of change a stronger, leaner, better business.

The lost art of sales

My father, Albert Hill, was a master of the art of selling. Always known as Dickie, my father spent most of his life working for my uncle, Arthur Fisher, in the family jewellery shop in Whangarei.

But even before Dickie came to the business, he was an accomplished salesman.

When he met my mother, Billie, my father was a charming,

handsome door-to-door salesman of Electrolux vacuum cleaners and the owner of an Oldsmobile sports car. He would knock on a door, invite himself in, vacuum the floor with whatever inferior instrument the family happened to own and then, with a flourish, unleash the Electrolux on all the dirt that was left behind. 'This filthy grime is all over your house,' he'd say, opening the Electrolux's dirt-choked bag with a look of discreet concern. His horrified clients would inevitably purchase.

With the patter and the look, Dickie was exactly the sort of chap you'd warn your daughter away from — but on the day he knocked in 1936, Billie was home alone. A few months later, they were married.

After a few years of marriage, Billie persuaded Dickie to give up travelling and to work for her brother Arthur in his jewellery shop, Fishers. Dickie was deft and capable, engraving watches and trophy cups and repairing jewellery — but his real talent was sales. He was a natural — charming and relaxed, warm and gregarious. Customers seemed to want to buy from him. His patter never seemed over the top or pushy, just calm and confident. He never bullied customers to buy, but equally he never let someone walk out of the shop before he had fully explored all possible desires their hearts might contain.

Dickie had countless cunning ideas for selling. His attention to detail was superb, as was his presentation of the jewels, his patter with the customer, his genuine desire to satisfy their shopping needs and, most importantly, his ability to close a deal.

Dickie understood how to make the experience pleasant for his customers. He never engaged in mindless banter. Rather, he sought to create a genuine engagement with everyone who came in the door. Dickie also knew how to upsell. Today, upselling is commonly understood to have something to do with asking if the customer wants fries with their burger — but in Dickie's case, it meant making extra sure that the item the customer purchased was the true fulfilment of their desires. Subtly and gently, Dickie

Dickie teaching me the art of selling, 1957.

would discover exactly what the customer was prepared to buy. He would never sell a plain silver ring if he thought there was any possibility the customer could be enticed to buy something more expensive.

And somehow, he would manage to avoid ever making a customer feel pressured or harassed. It's a gentle game, sales — if a salesman is too timid, he won't sell as much as he could. If he gives even a hint of pushiness or intimidation, he won't sell anything at all — or at the very least he won't get any returning customers. It's no good having customers purchase something just to get the salesman off their backs.

The key to Dickie's success was knowing his customers. His days as a travelling salesman were the most raw, real training he could possibly have — he didn't have the luxury of waiting for people to wander into his shop to buy something; he had to try and talk his way into their living rooms, and then (politely) refuse to leave until they had bought something. It was tough work, and there was nowhere to hide — if he was hopeless, he wouldn't even make it past the threshold.

Dickie brought those skills to the counter of Fishers — and that meant he avoided the classic weakness of shop salesmen. Many sellers who trained in shops were obsessed with the product. They were swept up in the magnificence of whatever it was they were selling — hats, wrenches, garden hoses — and assumed, at some level, that the products would sell themselves. All these people believed they had to do was display to the grateful buying public their wares, and the sale was done. Dickie knew that wasn't true. The selling process itself is always primary.

Dickie had gleaned, in his years of experience, that if you knew enough about your customer, the product was irrelevant. You could make a sale no matter what it was you were selling.

Part of Dickie's talent was in analysing why a sale went wrong. If someone came into the shop and he engaged them, asked them the right questions, showed them his wares, and yet they walked out without buying anything, Dickie would stage an action replay. He would get me or someone else to retrace the steps of the non-buying customer.

'Aha!' he'd declare at the point where the sale had gone wrong. 'Now I understand.' He would isolate the exact moment at which the customer lost interest and started heading for the door, and carefully unpick all the steps that led to that point — what he'd said, what the customer had said, and the most likely explanation for the disconnect. With the next customer, he would make sure none of the same mistakes were made.

It's common nowadays in shops to get the impression that staff don't care much whether a customer buys something or not. Back at Fishers, the sale was our reason for being — and if one of the team didn't feel the sale was going well, Dickie would be close at hand, leaning over in his friendly way to see if he could help. Invariably, he knew just the right thing to say to put a customer at ease and get the register ringing.

Many years after Dickie had taught me to sell, I found myself teaching his lessons to my own staff in my own shop, Michael Hill Jeweller, in Whangarei. I employed a young watchmaker, Mike Parsell, and a friend of ours, Howard Bretherton, who had owned Fast Eddie's burger bar in town and had a knack for retail.

To begin with, Howard, Mike and I all worked together on the floor in the Whangarei shop. I watched every move they made and, although I liked them both enormously on a personal level, I became the harshest critic each of them had ever known.

Each of us had our own sales style, and we competed fiercely. After each sale, we'd deliver a critique of where the other guy had gone wrong. We all gleefully waited for the others to make a mistake, so we could point it out to them. It sounds like male egos gone mad, but it was all in the cause of making ourselves better salesmen, and improving our business.

Our competitive spirit meant very few people got out of the shop without having bought something — and no matter how fierce the competition got, I always insisted the customer have a pleasant, memorable experience. There's no point making a sale if the customer has only bought something to shut you up. Sure, there's money in the till, but that customer will never return — and retail relies on the goodwill of our customers. You want people to like you.

At Michael Hill, as at Fishers, it was very important to me that the store was an inviting place. We wanted it to be a meeting place, a hub of the community. People would come in with morning tea, cakes and scones, and just stay for a chat. We might make them a cuppa and talk for a while and as well as making their day pass more happily, it meant there was always plenty of action.

When half the other shops in town were like morgues, ours

would be crammed with people. That meant passers-by were curious about the buzz, and would come in to investigate what was happening — and then we'd be even busier.

I also learned a lot about selling from a brilliant woman who worked with us, Joke (pronounced Yolka) Jansen, who was the person who insisted I interview Mike Parsell. She had come to Michael Hill with me from Fishers, and had a wonderful, natural technique.

Joke would sit on a stool behind the counter just inside the shop door, where customers would barely notice her, fussing around polishing jewel-

Joke Jansen, a great salesperson who knew just how to make a customer feel good about buying, circa 1979.

lery, or perhaps rearranging rings on a tray. When a customer came in, she'd make some friendly comment to attract their attention. She would never, ever say anything so gauche as 'Can I help you?', or 'If you see something you like, let me know.'

When I hear either of those phrases in shops today, I cringe. They are a complete waste of time; making customers feel edgy and set-upon. It's far better to do as Joke did — let the customers know you have noticed them and are attentive and interested — but never make them feel like you only care about them because they might buy something.

Selling is a human business. Our customers will only feel good about buying from us if they like the feeling they get in the store — and that means the relationship has to be about more than just commerce.

Joke rarely missed a sale.

If you want one year of prosperity, grow grain.
If you want ten years of prosperity, grow trees.
If you want a hundred years of prosperity, grow people.
Chinese proverb

Chapter 4

HUNT THE RIGHT PEOPLE AND HELP THEM BECOME BETTER

By now you'll be getting the picture. In countless ways, both cognitive and practical, I believe the downturn is not necessarily bad news for business. And here's the most important point of all: rising unemployment represents a golden opportunity. That might sound a bit hard-hearted, but I think bright, talented, enthusiastic people have nothing to fear from a recalibration of the job market. Here's why. Businesses of all kinds will take this as an opportunity to pare back their staff numbers, assessing who is working well and getting rid of the rest.

If you are running a business, it's a wonderful time to be looking for the right people. Suddenly, a great deal of potential staff will come onto the job market. There has been a marked skill shortage in so many professions, trades and occupations in the past decade or so, but now there will be a positive glut of people looking for work. And they'll be genuine jobhunters, too. I've often found that when a position is advertised, you'll get a certain number of applicants who are just tyre-kickers. They already have jobs, but they're looking around to determine whether they might be able to get a pay rise, or whether a job might be available if, in future, they decide to move on.

In a downturn, none of that applies. Everybody is conscious of the value of a job, and the very real danger of unemployment. When you post a job advertisement, you'll find all the applicants are genuinely on the market.

So make the most of this opportunity. At the same time as you are examining all the aspects of your business, you should be considering your overall headcount and your distribution of human resources. You may not necessarily need to reduce your staff numbers, but this could be a good time to redeploy staff who aren't suited to the positions in which they have found themselves. And even if you think your staff are doing well, it's a perfect moment to consider the kind of people who might be out there looking for work. Have any of your competitors closed or downsized? If so, consider which people may be presently between jobs. Could any of them suit your organisation? If so, you should do whatever it takes to get them — even if it means combining two positions into one, or merging a couple of departments to give the new person a workable and meaningful role. There's no danger in occasionally shaking up the way you do things if the payoff is so potentially great.

I believe it's far better to cause a little turmoil and get the right people if your alternative is putting up with average or sub-standard staff merely to avoid disruption. The benefit of bringing fresh people into your team will be immediate: as long as you are careful about the way you introduce new employees, and ensure nobody feels threatened or intimidated. You will find your brilliant new people can inspire and reinvigorate the whole team.

Why is this so important? Surely a well-run company, with clear workflows and effective structures, will hum along nicely no matter who is in what job, right? Wrong — completely. I really believe a team is only as strong as the mix of individuals within it, and that means your duty, as the boss, is to make sure everyone is in the right job, being used to the best of their abilities, constantly challenged and truly happy.

So how do you find the right people? How do you build the perfect team? And how do you identify who you need?

My approach has always been this: start with yourself. Assess your own strengths, and determine how your time can be best spent. And if you are honest about your strengths, you'll also be honest about your weaknesses. With a list of flaws and failings in front of you, the answers will pop out.

Let's take my own example. I'm a good salesman, thanks to the close tutelage of my brilliant father, Dickie. I'm good at ideas, and I'm comfortable with staff relations. Conversely, I'm not so hot on figures. I'm not the best person to be analysing balance sheets and devoting long periods to crunching numbers. So it's essential for me to find other people to do that stuff.

And here's the most important bit: always go in search of people who are smarter than you. The truly great managers are never afraid of having brilliant staff. Confident, assured managers know that clever employees make the whole team look good. There might be a bit of internal competition — but that's a good thing. You can make it work for you, as long as you're constantly ensuring that everyone is in a position that suits them, and in which they're being challenged.

There's no shame in using your team to cover your weaknesses. That, indeed, should be the whole idea. Take the example of a rugby team. If your first employee is a great fullback, there's no point hiring 14 other less-talented fullbacks: rather, you need a brilliant halfback, two sensational wingers, five enormous front-rowers and a pair of speedy flankers, as well as great centres and a decent first five-eighth. All of them should, ideally, be expert specialists, and if that's the case, the whole team will look good.

And that brings me to the second big point about talented employees: they will stimulate their colleagues and inspire the boss — you.

The journey of staffing doesn't end with finding the right team, of course. You need to be encouraging them all the way along. However, that doesn't mean just standing behind an employee's desk, saying: 'You're brilliant.' Sometimes, that's entirely the wrong thing to do. I spend a great deal of time telling my staff I think they're excellent, but I'm also prepared to have the tough conversations when necessary.

Here are a few of the conversations I've had in recent years.

I was visiting one of our regional stores and hopped in the car with one of our most brilliant young managers, a woman who has always been clearly on her way to big things within the organisation. She's energetic and vital and always positive — but I'd noticed over the previous few months that she had put on a lot of weight. I gradually worked the conversation around to her future.

'I want you to know I think you're amazing,' I said to her. 'You've done some fantastic work in the past few years. You're clever and talented and I think you have a great future with us. But I have to be honest with you: I'm concerned about your health.' I told her I'd noticed she had put on weight, and that I wanted to help her lose it. I said I would pay for a personal trainer for her, and that we would also cover the cost of consulting a nutritionist.

How did she react? Of course, she was embarrassed. She blushed and stammered and, for a few moments, it was very awkward. But as we continued driving, she took a big breath and told me she was glad I'd raised the issue with her. She said she was acutely conscious of her weight gain, but attributed it to a combination of long hours and difficult times at home. She said she'd be glad to take me up on the offer of a trainer — and her courage to reveal the issues she was experiencing allowed us to have a really honest and frank conversation about what was going on in her life.

I'm not pretending that these sorts of conversations will be easy. It's very hard to critique someone in a way that leaves them feeling good about themselves, and preserves a good relationship between the two of you.

Here's another example. We had another rising star who had just one big flaw — shockingly bad breath. Every time I spoke to him, I was conscious of a seriously bad smell emanating from his mouth. I could tell it wasn't just me who had noticed — when we were in a group discussion, I'd see people perceptibly recoiling a little as this particular fellow spoke. So I had a word to him about it, and again I prefaced my remarks with some comments about how great I thought he was.

'I've got to tell you,' I eventually said, 'you've got bad

breath. I'm sure you're not aware of it, but I'd want to know if it was me. I think you might need to make a quick trip to the dentist.' In the end, he had a dentist's assessment, and an awareness of dental hygiene did the trick.

Again, my young employee was initially embarrassed, but because I had been careful to couch my criticism in caring, thoughtful terms, he was ultimately pleased I had raised it. And when I told him that I was concerned his breath might hold him back, I was being honest — nobody is going to buy a piece of jewellery from a salesman who's breathing toxic fumes across the counter, and nobody's going to promote a person they can't bear to be in the same room with.

It's a bit like the old maxim about newsreaders: if you notice what they're wearing, they're wearing the wrong thing. Maintaining physical standards is not only a crucial part of sales; it's an essential element in successful business. So much of commercial relationships is founded on personal interaction and rapport, and if there's a big distracting factor, everyone's attention will be diverted to the wrong place.

On other occasions, I've confronted a staffer about his excessive drinking, and I've offered voice training to another manager to help him improve his sales performance.

In the case of the heavy drinker, it wasn't that he was violent or offensive when he was drunk, it was just that he was distracting everyone's attention from the best parts of his persona. After our big annual conferences, he would always be one of a hard-core crew who would kick on at the bars and clubs around town after the day's meetings had finished. The next day everyone would be talking about what this particular man had got up to the night before — which meant that nobody was really paying attention to what he was saying in his presentations. He was undermining his own brilliance with his nocturnal partying. So I took him aside for a quiet word, and told him how impressed I had been with his most recent presentation. I worked the conversation around to the fact that I, like everyone else in the company, had heard of his reputation as a party animal. I said I felt it was essential for him to get his drinking under control, and offered to help him by finding a good counselling service.

Of course, you can guess what came next. He was horrified that I had raised this issue with him, and dreadfully embarrassed to be confronted over what he thought was nothing more than an innocent penchant for good times. Once he was aware of the extent to which his behaviour was considered unusual, and that he was the subject of in-depth company discussion, he was even more appalled.

At the end of my spiel, he sat quietly for a moment and then came out with a startling announcement.

'I don't think I'll cut down my drinking,' he said. 'I'm going to give up altogether.'

He did, too. It's now been several years since he's had a drink. He has lost weight, become super-fit and is now realising his full potential as one of our most promising executives. It's been very exciting to watch — and it all came from that first difficult conversation.

So here's the message: whenever I deliver criticism, I make sure to wrap it in worthy praise, and to present a solution. It's crucial to do all those things in the same conversation. There's no point enumerating someone's faults if you aren't prepared to help them work their way out of the problems and towards a brighter future. If I'd just told our young female manager that she was overweight, or announced that I thought our young executive was in danger of becoming an alcoholic, nothing would have been achieved. Both those people would have been demoralised and depressed, and I'd have got no closer to a solution. But by making sure they both felt supported and encouraged, we got to keep them in the company and push them forward to a brighter future.

Sometimes, it can all seem too hard. We've all been confronted with staff or colleagues who seem to have serious problems of personality or behaviour. If their managers are impatient or intolerant, they'll lose their jobs. But does that help the problem? Not really. I think sacking a staffer should be the last resort. You owe it to your employees — and to your organisation — to try to improve the situation of individuals, and thus lift the whole team.

It comes back to the importance of having a vision. If you can help your staff member understand your vision for them — and how their flaw might be holding them back from achieving that vision — you can help to unlock a great future. There might not be much incentive to lose weight or give up drinking if the only reward is more of the same day-to-day work. But if you can sell the promise of a greater opportunity in the years ahead, you can show your staffer why change is necessary, and that's half the battle won.

Here's another example of how building a good team is good for you as a leader.

In the early 1980s, despite the speed at which we were expanding across New Zealand, we had a problem with our new store in Takapuna, on Auckland's North Shore. After the usual opening blast of publicity, the store was struggling. It was clear to Christine and me where the problem lay: our manager was a great guy, but he had trouble delegating and was doing too much himself. He spent all his time in the backroom worrying about orders and accounts and rosters, which meant he was never out the front of the store training

Mike Parsell (centre) and his team at Takapuna, Auckland, just before he left to set up the Australian branch, June 1987.

his staff in sales.

'You can stick these up your arse,' he told me after just a year, handing back the keys to the store. 'There's no money in this place. It'll only work as a watch shop.'

Did I take his advice? No, I did not. Because by then I had a secret weapon, a secret weapon I still have to this day.

His name is Mike Parsell, a brilliant manager who had been training in our Whangarei shop for just such an opportunity.

In the first week Mike was at Takapuna, turnover shot up 30 per cent, and within three years we were raking in $3.2 million each year. In 1986, that was an awful lot of money.

Here's why: Mike understood the importance of training a dedicated sales team. He knew how crucial it was for him to spend his days on the floor, overseeing trade and engaging with customers and staff. And, most importantly, Mike grasped the central truth of good management: delegation.

I have come to believe over the years that the key to success is to build a fabulous team, and then become coach of that team. A manager's time is best spent improving the performance of the team: fitting people into the jobs that suit them best, and then trusting them to get on with their tasks.

With perseverance, trust and the example of a passionate and dedicated leader, any team can learn to shine.

If I have a secret to success, that is it.

For me, it was the most important lesson to learn as a leader. Once I worked out what I wanted from my business life, I discovered the only way to achieve it was to find the right people and make them feel trusted and valued. This meant I could keep forming goals for myself, and have confidence they could be achieved.

Here's where I found Mike Parsell, several years earlier.

In our early days in Whangarei, I advertised for a trainee manager, offering a wage well above average for the time. I got a pile of applications, one of which came from a young man who described himself as a watchmaker.

'Watchmakers have tunnel vision,' I muttered to myself, putting Mike's application in the reject pile.

Fortunately, the office assistant was a smart young woman who knew better. She retrieved Mike's application and scheduled an interview. Still, I was reluctant, and sent one of our best salespeople, Joke Jansen, to talk to this pesky fellow.

'Michael,' said Joke after her talk with Mike, 'you have to talk to him. He's perfect.'

He was, too. Barely 20 years old, friendly and enthusiastic,

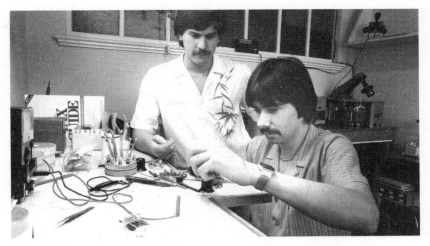
Our new watchmaker, Mike Parsell (front), with Laurie Mayo, 1981.

he was a self-taught watchmaker who fixed timepieces for all the stores in town, except ours. He was earning about $14,000 per annum and working 18-hour days. I was offering $40,000 — so he was keen to persuade me that he had the ability and potential I needed.

Hiring Mike was one of the best moves I ever made. I liked him instantly. I trusted him completely. And he proved over the years the immense benefit of listening to my instincts — hire people you like, and the personal rapport will carry you both a long way.

I installed Mike in the Whangarei shop doing watch repairs in the morning, then learning his way around the retail side of the business in the afternoon. Within weeks, he showed me he was a natural salesman, a fun and inspiring workmate, and a brilliant future leader. All the staff liked him. He was diligent and dedicated — and, most importantly, he was never threatened by other diligent, dedicated people. To the contrary, he always sought them out, and encouraged them. He knew they were essential for making the team, the business and Mike himself look good. There's nothing vain or silly about that — it's smart business.

Today, Mike is chief executive officer of Michael Hill International, and integral to our success. Thank goodness I listened to Joke.

Michael Hill staff story: Brenda Watson
Regional manager, South Australia

I was a newly appointed regional manager with a leading jewellery company in Australia, an appointment that I had worked hard towards for 10 years, when a phone call came from Cliff Mason, the manager of Michael Hill Belconnen, Canberra. He asked if I would like to meet to discuss a career change. My immediate response was a polite no; why would I consider moving from a company who was seen as the leading jeweller in the industry and who had just rewarded my commitment to them with my promotion?

One week later Michael Hill opened in Woden Plaza. I stood watching from the front of my store, which was empty due to the crowd of more than 300 people gathered outside the Michael Hill store, awaiting its opening. As I looked once more into my empty store, I realised, at that moment, I was working for the wrong company.

Two weeks later, I started my career with Michael Hill, the best career choice I have ever made. The excitement of working for such an innovative, people-focused, financially sound and powerful company has never diminished.

I take great pride in having played a part in developing the company in Canberra, Brisbane and Sydney. The highlight of my career to date was the exciting adventure assisting Emma Hill in establishing Michael Hill in Canada.

I strive to always surround myself with smart, talented people who can go as far as they desire. I am always aware that people need a goal to galvanise them and that talented people will always strive to find a way to make their dreams happen.

After 16 years, I feel as excited and focused as on my first day, and I am sure that Michael Hill will become the number one international jewellery brand in the world.

Michael Hill staff story: Angie Hardy
Diamond-buyer, Australia

I started in the manufacturing department of Michael Hill Brisbane, which had a staff of only six. I was ordering the diamonds and coloured gemstones for the production jewellery for the 14 stores we then had in Australia. I was probably ordering five–10 carats of diamonds weekly, whereas now, after nearly 18 years, I currently purchase up to 18,000 carats, which equates to 300,000 diamonds annually. Over the years we have built up our workshop to a staff of 50 and we are the largest jewellery manufacturer in Australasia.

Diamond-buying is an art and it's also a tough world. With such high standards set by the company there is no room for error. I always have to be on the top of my game when it comes to checking quality and, because the market changes constantly, ensuring we are getting the best product at the best price.

Overall my journey with Michael Hill has been full of amazing insights. I have been given such fantastic opportunities to grow and so have given my utmost to the company in return. I always want to give 110 per cent. I am still learning so much and love what I do.

Michael Hill staff story: Renaye Huia
Store manager, Brisbane

I started part-time with Michael Hill until a manager-in-training (MIT) role came up. After maternity leave and more part-time work I was full-time and eventually became a store manager.

I then set myself a goal to become the best store manager

with the best store. Brett Halliday was a great mentor and I thank him for being as tough as he was. It has made me strong.

I am now the manager of the leading store in Queensland.

It is a great reward to watch team members become top sellers in the company, watching my MIT become a store manager and watching my team help me achieve my dream. The highlight was winning Trainer of the Year, as it recognised my desire to give back what others have done for me, and watching other team members' dreams come true.

My heart still lies in helping a customer fulfil their dream of owning a beautiful piece of jewellery. And my ultimate goal is to keep loving my job.

Michael Hill staff story: Rimma Mulligan
Sales professional, Manukau

I come from Russia and immigrated to New Zealand. I am very lucky to have been a part of a great team at Manukau for the past 11 years. I have been working mostly part-time while raising a young family of three boys, the eldest of whom is now 15 and the youngest seven.

I have a great passion for my job, I'm extremely driven and I thrive on a challenge. Michael Hill Jeweller has guided me and given me the right tools for selling, and together with my personality this creates the right chemistry to produce great results. I have always been one of the top sales professionals in the store. I find it invigorating to help people find that special piece of jewellery that complements their personality and lifestyle.

In early March 2008, the company launched a worldwide challenge for the first sales professional to reach $1 million in sales to win a BMW Series 3. I took a copy of the email home to my husband Mike, and we made a chart to set weekly and monthly goals to reach this target. I was very excited and confident I could do it. In 2007 I had broken the record for the highest amount of sales which was $764,000 and we calculated that I had to do $20,000 a week in order to win the prize.

The final results were amazing. I managed to reach $1,108,000 for the year in sales and won the BMW! Wow!

It was truly an unforgettable moment. My family and my husband were so proud. I was overwhelmed and humbled by the huge support and recognition I received from the company, friends and family.

In the middle of difficulty
lies opportunity.
Albert Einstein

Chapter 5

GET DOWN TO THE COALFACE

Let's play a little game. Think of the youngest, newest employee in your company, and picture him or her going about the first tasks of the workday, whether it's vacuuming the carpet or ringing a supplier or going through the overnight emails. Got a mental picture? Great. Now think of the farthest corner of your business — whether it's a regional office in the backblocks of Somewheresville, or just the darkest, furthest corner of your little shop.

You should know exactly what is happening in both of those environments. A good businessperson knows precisely what's happening in the most distant, least-noticed sector of the company — and a really great entrepreneur is able and willing to step in and do the job of just about anyone in the business, whether it's the delivery driver or the salesperson.

Over the years, I have watched too many companies allow head office to suck all the attention away from the real business — like a giant black hole at the centre of the solar system, consuming all the light and energy.

In a time of economic downturn, that tendency becomes particularly pertinent. How much time are the executives spending behind their desks in some industrial park, or on the top floor of a city building, while the real workers toil away, unseen and forgotten?

It's a strange habit, but I've seen it extending across most businesses, and I hear it in the conversations I have with CEOs and executives all the time. It's part of our human tendency to become wrapped up in the tasks directly in front of us: we sit there gazing into our computers, or looking down at our desks, and before we know it the day has passed and we've failed to connect with the real world.

In a big business, it is characterised by a particular kind of amnesia. What is it we do again? What do we make? What do we sell? If the senior managers and executives are spending all their time thinking about key performance indicators and balance sheets, no wonder they can't remember the important stuff.

And although it might be easy for bosses to forget what's going on, the employees don't have a chance to forget: they're enmeshed in that business, every day, and they'll be increasingly aware of the gulf between themselves and the executives.

And they'll certainly be aware that the executives don't have a clue. Stop an office worker in the street, or a factory hand, and ask how often they've met their chief executive officer. Most of them wouldn't even know the CEO's name, although they might have heard a whisper about how much he or she gets paid. Not a good look.

Christine and I have always made a point of visiting our stores on a regular basis. Whenever we're in a city, we'll set aside a day to visit all the Michael Hill Jeweller shops and talk to the staff. We'll stand behind the counter with the salespeople and talk to the customers. I remember during one visit, Christine grabbed a cloth and started wiping some fingerprints off a glass window. One of the young sales assistants was horrified: the boss, cleaning a window? But that's just the way we work. Our business philosophy has always been that nobody in the company — absolutely nobody — is too busy or important to clean a window.

We're lucky, in some ways, that the business evolved slowly and organically. I wasn't hired by some recruitment firm to run a 100-store business that already existed; we built it up, store by store. So it's always been a natural thing for Christine and me to know where each of the stores is, and to visit them regularly. I know that when an executive is hired by a company, life can suddenly be crammed with a million essential tasks, all of which need to be conducted in head office. But I can't emphasise too strongly the importance of getting down to the scene of the real action: it's the only way to really understand a business. A competent executive should never be surprised by the latest sales figures, or the news that staff turnover has suddenly rocketed up since the last quarter. Any boss who is plugged in will have heard the word long before it is reflected in financial data, because he or she will have been on the shop floors, or talking to the distribution centre, and be well aware that sales are slower this week than they were last week, for example.

And in a well-managed company, that philosophy should extend all the way down the chain. Think about a typical

Top left: Christine with Ray Arminger, who rebuilt our house after the fire and then built our stores.
Top right: Preparing our new-look Whangarei store with Mark and Emma, 1979.
Bottom: After buying Keith's shop, Garlands, in Hastings, 1981. From left: Christine, Keith Garland, Sid Cole, Mary Muir and me.

work environment — an office, a factory or a shop. If a phone is ringing and ringing at an empty desk, does anyone pick it up? If a visitor comes in through the door, do they stand around looking lost for ages before anyone deigns to approach and ask if they need help?

There are too many occasions when staff think they can't do certain tasks because 'it's not my job', or focus on their own duties without lifting their heads to see if anyone else needs help.

And again, it all comes back to a fundamental understanding of the question: what are we really doing here? In our case, the answer is clear: buying and selling jewellery.

That's what everything comes back to. Our core business is not writing annual reports, or talking about strategy, or sending emails, although that stuff all has to be done as well. But it's a sideline to the real business. The important thing is that we constantly remind ourselves what it's all for, the fundamental purpose that we're all driving towards.

There's no better way to jog the memory than cleaning a shop window, and talking to the staff while you're doing it.

Christine sums it up well: 'Our staff don't work for us,' she says, 'they work with us.' At every level of the business, she knows who is who, and she always knows what they do. And what's more, she's glad to help if she can.

I'm not suggesting we're perfect, by the way. The only reason I'm so convinced of this point is that we've learned from our mistakes — from doing things the other way, the wrong way.

In the early 1990s, once we had made the decision to close our Whangarei head office and concentrate on Brisbane, we put our chief executive, Mike Parsell, in charge of creating a new headquarters in Queensland. It was to be a purpose-

MHJ, new head office in Brisbane, 2001.

built structure, with distribution and manufacturing all on the same site. Mike did it — there's not much he can't do — at the same time as running the rest of the company.

But it came at a cost.

During the time Mike was looking for land, meeting with real estate people, talking to developers, considering plans and deciding upon structures, the rest of the business suffered. Our retail figures across the group were not as strong. And once we realised this, it was easy to see why.

'We've turned the grandstand around,' I said to Mike. 'We've turned our backs on the playing field.'

What I meant was this: the stores are our main business, and should be the main focus for our CEO.

But we had distracted Mike with a massive task that should have been delegated to others. It was wrong to think that he could maintain his close focus on the retail side of the business at the same time as playing property developer.

And guess what? Once we restored the balance and allowed Mike to get back to doing his real job, retail recovered. He was able to attend to all the pressing details of the business that we needed him to focus on, and the problem was solved.

To continue the playing-field metaphor for a moment, Mike was now able to see who was kicking goals, and who needed to be taken off the bench and sent into the game.

'What is our business?' we asked ourselves — and the answer made it all clear. Not building offices. Not thinking about truck-parking bays or development approvals. We are buyers and sellers of jewellery.

Now we've established why it's important to get down to the coalface, let me tell you how astonished I am when I talk to some of the people who want jobs with our company.

'Corporate strategy is my main interest,' they might say, or: 'I've spent four years studying human resources and I'm across all the latest theories.'

They seem to have visions of spending the rest of their days in a corporate office somewhere, wearing sharp suits and saying important-sounding things to one another.

Frankly, that doesn't impress me. I don't want people whose experience consists of several semesters sitting in a business studies lecture theatre. I want people who are prepared to get behind a shop counter and understand how a business really works, people who want to learn the business from the shop floor up.

If they're not prepared to do that, they're not right for our company.

And here's the key point: retail is a great sector for people who want a brilliant executive career. Too often, I think retail is overlooked by bright young people with an interest in business. They think the only way to get ahead and forge the sort of business career they want is to get a job at a big accountancy firm, or a giant human resources conglomerate, or a beverage behemoth, dreaming up the latest flavour of fizzy chemical-water and marketing it to teenagers.

That's a shame, for I believe retailing is a fascinating, diverse and dynamic business. There's plenty of scope for creativity and big-picture thinking and ambition. There are countless fascinating careers in the retail sector, but I've met plenty of young people who regard shops with the hint of a sneer around the corners of their mouths.

'Oh yes,' they seem to be saying, 'but retail's not real business, is it?'

Well, yes it is. It's about as real as you can get: it's about understanding human beings on all sorts of levels, from staff to customers and everyone in between. And it's about working out what people want, and forging relationships with them. To get a grasp on that, I believe it's crucial to get onto the shop floor and learn how to sell something.

If you're afraid to get down to the coalface, it's not the right business for you. But if you can taste the thrill of building a giant multinational company from a single shop, come and talk to us: we're always looking for the right people.

For me, making a sale is the best feeling imaginable. I love walking into a store, saying hello to a customer and watching them walk out a little while later with a neatly wrapped parcel in a Michael Hill Jeweller bag.

Life changed for me when I learned about the magic of retail.

As a young man, once it was clear my dream of being a professional violinist wasn't going to fly, my uncle Arthur decided I was to be put to work in the family business, where my father and mother also worked.

'You're going to be a watchmaker, son,' Uncle Arthur said.

Oh dear. I had no interest in watches, or clocks. Suddenly I could see my future shrinking down to the size of the microscopic cogs and springs I was to spend the rest of my life fixing. What a nightmare.

In a room out the back of Fishers were seven full-time watchmakers. It might be hard to believe, by today's standards — today you wouldn't find a single watchmaker

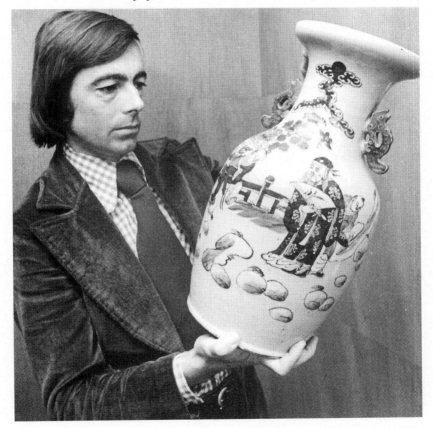

Fishers the Jewellers also carried antiques. Here, I am appraising a Chinese vase, 1970.

in most jewellery shops — but watchmaking was a huge business back then. Every watch and clock was a delicate, fragile little piece of machinery, which meant they always needed fixing.

There was more than enough work to keep seven people employed and I was to be the eighth. My uncle sat me at the end of this big long bench next to Norman Wright, the head of watchmaking.

The first day, Norman started me on uncollected repairs. The premise seemed to be that as no one had come to pick these things up, no one would care if they weren't properly fixed. He brought out a Big Ben alarm clock, unscrewed the back and took out all the innards.

'There you are, you put it together again,' he said, and strode off.

I sat there in horror. I simply did not have a clue about what to do.

Norman probably wasn't a great teacher but I was no doubt an awful student. I just looked at this pile of bits and pieces, appalled at what my life had become. There seemed to be dozens of tiny cogs with brass ends. Someone eventually came and told me they needed to be turned on a lathe, which I could do without too much trouble. My real problem was the minuscule hair springs, which are responsible for making a clock go tick-tock. I couldn't seem to keep my hands on them. They sprang and bounced all over the place like they were in a cartoon.

Somehow, I got all the pieces back inside the clock, and it appeared to work. Eventually, I graduated to Baby Ben alarm clocks, which were smaller and even more fiddly. Later, I moved on to men's watches, a development that did not make me popular with my colleagues. I spent more time asking for help and watching other people correct my mistakes than I spent actually fixing watches.

The next stage was ladies' watches, which were really tiny in those days. I could see my world getting smaller and smaller — and it was not a good feeling.

As I was part of the family, Norman had to persevere with me, but he knew, as did I, that I had no aptitude or inclination for repairing watches. Finally, it became too much for his patience, and Norman went to my uncle.

'We can't have him here, we have to get him out, he's wrecking too many watches,' he told Arthur.

Arthur sighed and made a decision — he would put me in the front of the shop with my dad, and we could sell together.

That decision changed everything.

The following morning, I arrived at work and was handed a broom. My first job was to sweep out the shop, then collect the mail, and then help with the window displays. It was infinitely better than continuing to botch watch surgery, and it was the beginning of a skill I could really get the hang of.

Dickie was to teach me the art of selling — and to give me a passion for the shopfloor that has never dissipated.

Michael Hill staff story: Greg Smith
Retail general manager, New Zealand

It was 1992 and I was 19 years old, and I had embarked on several government-funded courses to fuel my surfing habit. The last, ironically, was a sales and marketing course.

While browsing in a Michael Hill store, daydreaming of getting engaged, I was approached by the trainee manager in the store and asked if I had ever considered a career in jewellery. I hadn't.

However, earning $8.50 an hour, 40 hours per week, was double my current income! I was flattered by the offer and invited the manager to lunch the next day to discuss what I would need to do to get the job. Go to the library and learn about diamonds was her answer.

I was fortunate the trainee manager saw something in me, or was it that I had offered to work for free for two weeks to prove I could do the job? Either way, I was in.

And so it began. The role of trainee manager could be best described as general dogsbody and my manager, Grant, reminded me of this often. It was the best training in the world, though; I learned the value of cleaning, writing clearly on a blackboard, making coffee and, finally, selling. Watches came first — they would not let me loose on the diamond clients. Fair enough — I could not tell the difference between a diamond and a sapphire. It was some kind of apprenticeship and I was proud to have the keys to a million-dollar store. My career was set to take off.

Carla, my ever-supportive wife, and I would spend the next 10 years in seven locations from Auckland to Invercargill. Then I was promoted to regional manager in the central North Island, managing 17 stores. Four years later, I was regional manager of South Australia and now I am retail general manager of New Zealand.

Throughout my time with Michael Hill Jeweller I have been trained, pushed, promoted and paid more than I could have imagined and yet, even today, more than ever, I can't wait to get up and come to work. Cheerleader? You bet. Is there more to come? You bet. Watch this space!

Michael Hill staff story: Brett Halliday
Retail general manager, Canada

When I was asked to join Michael Hill Jeweller in 1993, with no retail or jewellery experience, my aim was to attain sales skills and business knowledge. After a few short months I found myself immersed in a culture of enthusiasm, passion and excitement as the company had started to grow quite rapidly. It was made very clear to me that there would be an abundance of opportunities and a bright future for anyone who wanted to work hard and embrace the company's values and vision.

I started as a trainee manager in Canberra, and then moved to Queensland to be a store manager. Then I was offered the opportunity to relocate to Perth, Western Australia, as the regional manager, to continue our expansion by opening new stores in this new market. Next, the chance to pack up the family once again and move across the world to Canada and continue the Michael Hill vision in another country was one of the greatest challenges that could be presented to anyone. To take on such an enormous task demands a great deal of support, not only from all of the different departments throughout the company, but also from a very strong, unselfish and perceptive family.

Michael Hill staff story: Phil Taylor
Chief financial officer

My introduction to the culture of Michael Hill Jeweller was back in December 1986 at the Whangarei head office when I was interviewed by Wayne Butler, the financial controller, and Howard Bretherton, the general manager — both were wearing Hawaiian shirts!

I started work with Michael Hill in January 1987 as the financial controller for Australia. Things moved quickly and in August that year I moved to Australia with the Hill family and Mike Parsell and his family to establish the Australian operation. It was a fast learning curve for me, never having worked in the retail industry before. However, one thing that never changes for me from one business to the next is the importance of getting to know the operation from the coalface out. I spent many hours and days helping to open those first few stores in Brisbane.

As a financial controller for the Australian operation, it was imperative that I understood the drivers of the business and that I could relate this to my role. I worked side by side with Mike Parsell, the general manager of the Australian business, and developed a strong grasp of what made the tills ring and what disciplines were required to crack a large market like Australia. First and foremost, finding the 'right' people for our company and looking after them was the key to our early success in Australia.

We had a lot of fun in those early years, because if things didn't go as planned, we had the attitude of 'nothing ventured, nothing gained'. The team at head office was small and effective, and we could move very quickly to address problems or seize opportunities. For many years we had just a handful of staff so everyone was in touch with the retail stores and we all spent time in the stores learning and helping.

Now, 22 years on, we have 140 stores in Australia and 250 stores worldwide.

The thing I have really enjoyed about my time with Michael Hill is the degree of independence that Michael and the board allow the management to have, and their willingness to listen to our thoughts and concerns. We always get a fair hearing at board meetings and they have an environment of openness, which has been a motivating factor for me over the years.

The one who asks a question
is a fool for five minutes,
the one who does not ask a
question is a fool forever.
Chinese proverb

Chapter 6

EMBRACE MISTAKES

Mistakes, I've made a few. I have been too trusting at times. I have allowed my enthusiasm to carry me away. I've made the wrong assumptions, hired the wrong people and tried to do too much, too soon.

But one mistake I have never made is regretting my mistakes.

Central to my philosophy of business is the firm belief that it is essential to make mistakes — and to learn from them. I have made countless errors in the course of creating and developing Michael Hill Jeweller, but I wouldn't have it any other way.

There's only one sure way to avoid mistakes altogether: never take a risk. I believe error-free business is a sure sign you're not pushing yourself hard enough. It might seem counter-intuitive, but it is the central truth of my business experience.

When we first crossed the Tasman to set up our business in Australia, we bungled and blundered repeatedly. Each time, we capitalised on our losses and turned them into positives. I believe that practice has made us strong — and we have never made the same mistake twice. That is the crux of this belief: mistakes are only positive if you are able to honestly recognise and assess them, then ensure they never happen again.

Our move to Australia in 1987 was thrilling. We sold the Whangarei house to a very flash American, Ronald Barnett, and packed up our lives to move to Brisbane. We quickly learned how little we knew about doing business in another country. Although Australia was physically close, the business culture was very different from New Zealand's, as we discovered to our cost.

Just getting started was a struggle. Our first battle was trying to lease a shop in any of the city's big shopping centres. Nobody had heard of Michael Hill Jeweller except the New Zealanders living in Brisbane — and I guess they thought the company might not last.

We didn't let it bother us too much, however, and just kept pushing our case with the shopping centres. We put together an immaculate presentation about the business, including photos of stores and samples of our advertisements, and showed it to the centre managers. Finally, we persuaded one manager to take a gamble on us, and he leased us two shops in the suburban centres of Chermside and Indooroopilly.

Both stores opened on 1 October 1987, 10 years to the day since the house fire. We went big with loss leaders: I appeared on television, advertising a sapphire and diamond ring worth $750 knocked down to $395. I think we made about $20, if

The Myer Centre store in central Brisbane — it was the flashest retail building built in the city at that time. This photo was taken for the 1993 Christmas catalogue.

that, but it got the crowds in and the place went ballistic. At the time, I was the only businessman in Brisbane presenting his own TV adverts, and it took everyone by surprise.

After the stores had been humming along for a few months, a site came up in the Myer Centre in central Brisbane. It was the flashest building in the city. The landlord promised we would be practically the only jewellers in the centre but there turned out to be several, plus there was a ratchet clause which hiked the rent up every year so that by the time our lease was out, we were paying well above market value.

Welcome to Queensland. It wasn't the same as doing deals on a handshake, the way we had in New Zealand. But here in Australia, we were an unknown company with no clout. We were in a whole new league.

It was a good lesson and one we could afford to learn at that time: read the fine print. Now we have all our contracts closely scrutinised by lawyers. We go through every detail, looking for traps, and we always make sure we are completely happy with an agreement before we sign.

Head office team in 1990: Mike Parsell, Phil Taylor, me and Christine.

With the small team of managers and trainees we had brought from New Zealand, we ran the business from our new head office on the eleventh floor of the swish IBM building on Edward Street, in the central business district. The surrounds were plush, but we couldn't quite afford furniture in the beginning; we worked on piles of telephone books instead of desks. Nobody cared. We wanted to conquer Australia, just as we had New Zealand.

Our crew was tight, and we had a great sense of camaraderie, but I was learning another lesson about transplanting staff into a foreign environment: only the toughest survive. Our early days in Australia proved such hard work that many of our imported New Zealand employees gave up and went home. I soon realised it was easier and better to employ and train locals who knew the Aussie culture rather than import our own expats — although the New Zealanders were well-versed in the Michael Hill Jeweller culture, many of them were totally lost in the Australian business scene.

What I really needed were talented people who were already well attuned to the local culture — and I found a perfect specimen completely by chance one day. The business was going so well I had decided to buy myself a Mercedes, and one day I found myself in the mid-sized regional city of Ipswich, west of Brisbane, where we were opening a store. I dropped into the Mercedes dealership and the salesman was so good that I went home with a new car and a new employee. I offered him a job on the spot, and he became a great manager.

That's the way I often acquired staff. There's nothing like finding out first-hand if they're any good. You can put all the ads you like in the paper or on the internet these days, but you find much better people just by looking for someone doing an exceptional job and offering them a position.

As I mentioned, I was fronting our television advertisements myself, as I had in New Zealand. There was another mistake: we made the ads far too wacky to begin with. In New Zealand the ads had changed gradually from conservative to out-there, and when we arrived in Australia, we assumed the crazy, idiosyncratic ads would work just as well as they did at home. We were wrong. Instead of regarding Michael Hill Jeweller as an exciting new concept in jewellery, many viewers thought I was a shonky used-car salesman.

Me in the TV studio, 1987.

In one ad I wore a business suit and was fully submerged in Brisbane's Olympic diving pool,

Shooting a TV commercial underwater in Brisbane's Olympic diving pool, 1991.

with a diver holding me below the surface and a cameraman shooting through the pool's porthole windows. In another ad, I emerged from the surf, dripping wet, again wearing a business suit. The ads grabbed attention and sparked sales, but my credibility was poor with the public — especially in conservative markets like Canberra, where they simply weren't used to outlandish TV advertising.

Canberra was a lesson in itself. After a few years in Brisbane, we decided to expand to the national capital, assuming its smallish size and affluent population would be perfect for our brand. We were right in some ways, but it proved to be simply too far away to be practical. At the time, there was no direct flight from Brisbane to Canberra, so we had to fly all our people and stock via Sydney, a time-consuming and expensive practice, with inevitable delays and missed connections. Servicing the Canberra market became difficult and bothersome, and drained far too much energy from the hub of our operation.

We should have been far more disciplined in our approach, focusing on growing the Michael Hill brand more quickly and effectively in Brisbane, instead of darting around the country. It's another mistake we have been careful not to repeat: now, when we enter a new market, we ensure the business is solid and stable in our first location before trying to expand.

Again, Winston Churchill's famous advice to never expose yourself on two fronts at the same time proved true. It was the perfect summation of our early Australian experience — and I'm thankful that we made that mistake at an early point in our international development. We were small and tough, and we could afford to make mistakes. From that day on we have always consciously kept warfare in mind when considering expansion — systematically take one city at a time.

Here's another mistake that taught us a hell of a lot: our disastrous attempt to branch into shoe retailing in 1992. As we settled into the business in Australia, working out neat systems for setting up shops on both sides of the Tasman and slowly expanding the business, two of our board members came up with a bright idea. Howard Bretherton and Johnny Ryder suggested we go into the shoe business.

They had met a Christchurch businessman, Peter Shaw, who had three high-end women's shoe shops. He was a good retailer, and Howard and Johnny thought we should buy the shops.

'That's crazy,' I said. 'What do we know about shoes?'

My reluctance didn't impress the others, but despite my reservations we went ahead. The whole thing turned out to be a series of colossal mistakes.

The first was that we allowed Howard to continue running the New Zealand jewellery stores, as well as looking after the shoe shops.

Not a success story: Michael Hill Shoes, 1992.

That was foolish: the shoes distracted Howard from his key business of running the jewellery stores, and the jewellery stores distracted him from getting a grip on the strange new world of shoes.

Our idea was that we would focus on the mass market, opening several middle-range shoe shops when we could. But what we failed to remember was that Peter Shaw's shops were renowned for high-quality, fashionable Italian footwear. In other words, we were taking Peter away from what he was good at, and launching him and an unknown product into a different market. It was very difficult for Peter to change his style — that was our second mistake.

The third mistake was that we opened nine shoe shops in quick succession, spread from Invercargill to Dunedin to Christchurch to Auckland, instead of concentrating on getting one area right before expanding further afield. The geographical distance meant we spread ourselves too thin. We had to advertise separately in each different region, which was costly. Transporting shoes and storing them is hugely expensive, quite unlike jewellery, which is immensely portable. Shoes take up a great deal of room — and we needed to buy dozens of sizes in each style.

The fourth mistake was naming the stores Michael Hill Shoes and locating them adjacent to the Michael Hill jewellery stores, thereby confusing the public. The TV commercials were even more confusing — if I was Michael Hill *Jeweller*, how could I be Michael Hill Shoes as well?

All this might sound obvious, but they were all factors we failed to properly consider before launching ourselves into it. We were out of our depth — and we didn't leave Peter to do his own thing, valuing him as the expert he was. A chain of high-end Peter Shaw shoe shops just might have worked. A

The big shoe clearance — me on top of shipping containers filming the last shoe advert for TV, 1994.

chain of Michael Hill mid-end shoe shops did not.

Howard and Peter Shaw had a tricky relationship, exacerbated by the vast differences between their areas of expertise. Shoes are much more of a fashion item than jewels, for instance, and styles change dramatically and rapidly. It's possible to predict jewellery trends, because the changes are usually subtle — but with shoes, the changes were horrifyingly quick. They went from very thin heels to platforms to stepladders in the blink of an eye.

We'd have clodhoppers arriving in vast numbers, but as soon as they arrived, they were going out of fashion — or the popular styles would sell out immediately and we'd be left with the dregs. At least with jewellery, if things go really bad, it's possible to melt the rings and necklaces down and start again — but with shoes, there's no going back.

It was very hard for us to determine exactly what the problem was, and the tensions were building. I was spending more and more time in the studio, trying to make better and more appropriate TV advertisements to rescue things, but the shoes still weren't selling. We were redesigning the shops, retraining the staff, analysing everything we could — but nothing improved.

In fact, things were getting worse. The jewellery business was starting to level off in New Zealand, although it was still developing well in Australia. In February 1994, two years after we had decided to get into shoes, we decided to pull out. We had nine shoe shops, and by June, we'd got rid of them all.

The final ad for Michael Hill Shoes was me on top of a large container saying, 'Hello, Michael Hill Shoes. I am quitting this container full of shoes at never-to-be-repeated prices. Everything must go.'

We were lucky to get out when we did. A failure like that can sometimes destroy an entire business.

There were some good things that emerged from the shoe disaster, however. Some of the best staff we have today, including Darcy Harkins, were junior staff in the shoe days — and now they're at the top of the business.

We lost a huge amount of money, but we learned some valuable lessons:

Keep it simple and stick to what you know and do best.

We can open thousands of jewellery shops — so why waste time on something we know little about?

Learn from Winston Churchill's wartime experience: don't engage on two fronts.

And never, ever, distract your key staff with irrelevancies.

Even with the best preparation, intentions and attitude, we still make mistakes at Michael Hill Jeweller. We're very good at dealing with them, however. I believe that if you're not making the odd mistake, you're too cautious. Christine has a rhyme she often repeats, which I think says it all:

There was a very cautious man who never laughed or cried.
He never won, he never lost, he never even tried.
And when at last he passed away his insurance was denied.
Because he never really lived, he never really died.

To this day, our attitude is that it's fine to make mistakes — as long as you don't make the same mistake twice. And always find a positive from the negative experience. If you are moving quickly, you'll come up against obstacles and difficulties — of course you will. It's how you deal with them that makes the difference.

Michael Hill staff story: Darcy Harkins

General manger, USA

I started with Michael Hill 17 years ago when I joined the short-lived Michael Hill Shoes company. I was selling shoes in a small store in Takapuna, Auckland. Most of my friends were at university and probably thought that working in a shop, selling shoes, would never amount to much.

Let me tell you, Michael Hill does not mess around! If you want to know why the company is successful, it is because it is an organisation of driven individuals that have a common goal in mind. When you become resilient enough to grow from the ongoing development and criticism, you fast become a much stronger individual. In no time at all, I found myself heading off to Christchurch to run my first store.

Unfortunately, my first stint at managing was rather brief, because the company decided that the shoe business was distracting them from the real game and Michael Hill Shoes was brought to an end. I moved into the jewellery company and then I really learned what a sales culture was. Michael Hill is a company that knows how to work hard, play hard and celebrate success, which I believe is part of the company's enormous culture of success.

I ran three stores in New Zealand. My first really big break was when Mike Parsell gave me the opportunity to be the first regional manager of Western Australia. Eighteen months later I was running Victoria and after four successful years I returned to New Zealand as the general manager.

Now we are in the great city of Chicago, launching the Michael Hill brand in the US. What a ride! Michael Hill has certainly given me the opportunity to achieve my dreams. The company has moulded and pushed me, held me back and sometimes kicked me, good and hard, in the backside. The rewards are as great as the work I have put in. Like many companies, some days are tough but we have a culture like none I have yet come across. I guess it's the same fighting spirit Michael put into the company on the day he started it.

Michael Hill staff story: Galina Hirtzel

Group diamond-buyer

I have worked for Michael Hill for half of my life. My career began

17 years ago when, like all other broke university students, I needed a part-time job. I was hired at the Queen Street branch on $10 an hour. Upon graduating, the reality soon hit that job prospects for a 19-year-old with a degree in romance languages weren't exactly falling off trees. So I thought I would kill a year until I turned 20 and join the Queen Street team full-time. The plan back then was to flit off to Europe and become an interpreter for the United Nations or something. Well, I never did get around to leaving. Oh, and I stayed on $10 an hour for a long, long time.

I soon came to realise that that was the way things were at Michael Hill. You worked hard and made sales, and hoped one day to get a store of your own. That was when you hit paydirt. I had heard rumours of what some of the managers earned and it dawned on me that I could have a great career right here at Michael Hill. I had met Michael and Christine, and felt that I was part of something really special. Under the tutelage of Kathryn Scott I started my campaign to become a manager; boy, did I have a lot to learn. I got my first store when I was a naive 22-year-old and soon started to learn about business Michael Hill style — sales, targets, expenses, gross profit, net profit all became part of my vernacular.

I moved cities a couple of times in pursuit of bigger, better stores and in 2002 I became New Zealand product manager, which required a move to Whangarei — not that easy a change for a city girl from Auckland. Then in 2004 I moved to Brisbane to the very best job of all, group diamond-buyer. I am responsible for the diamond jewellery category which contributes 50 per cent of the company's sales and is growing. It is an incredible privilege to hold this role and one that many people no doubt covet. It certainly sounds very glamorous, but when you are responsible for spending $100 million of the company's money every year it also comes with a lot of pressure. But I do relish it and love nothing more than seeing the product I have selected sell and make the company a lot of money. Sure, I have made my share of mistakes (some I'll never live down) but I have learned from them, and over the years my confidence has grown immensely.

The last five years have been the best of my career. I have been on a very steep learning curve and I still keep discovering new things about the diamond game. It is a large, complicated and fickle industry that is constantly changing. At the end of the day diamonds and gold are commodities that are subject to volatile market forces like any others. Added to all that, the need to think in four currencies — it definitely keeps me on my toes. This current economic climate makes my job even more challenging, as we strive to source better product at better prices. I have to be smart, strong and confident to do this well — not to mention a tough little negotiator.

I never did get to the United Nations to use my languages, but you know what? I wouldn't change a thing.

Michael Hill staff story: Tony Lum
Training and communications manager

Fifteen years ago, I set forth on an amazing journey. I have always wanted a career that would allow me to travel internationally. So the first step in my master plan was to complete a degree in international business. I then looked for my very first position in the corporate world. And, just like thousands of graduates before me, I discovered that my bachelor's degree was not the ticket to the corporate domination I had hoped for.

In a matter of weeks I had gone from corporate domination to desperation — I needed a job, any job. Luckily I had worked in retail while completing my degree and the jewellery company I had worked for offered me a cadetship. Within a few months I worked my way from sales assistant to assistant manager. On my first day as assistant manager, I had the wind knocked out of my sails. My new manager informed me that I would not get any further in the company, as someone needed to die before I would be promoted — so much for nurturing a young man's career aspirations!

Funnily enough, a friend was working at Michael Hill and told me that if I really wanted a career that I should apply for a position with them. During my interview, along with 25 other people, we were told that Michael Hill would be expanding internationally and that as a company they prided themselves on training and developing future talent. My international career plans were back on the horizon.

Eight hours later, when the interview had finished, I walked out hoping to God that I had outperformed the other 24 candidates. Four days later I got the phone call I was waiting for, and so my journey began.

Within six months I had gone from manager-in-training to the manager of my very first store. I was 21, earning twice as much as all of my friends, and I was determined to be the next regional manager in no time flat.

It's funny how fate intervenes: my first foray into management was not as smooth as I had thought it would be. In eight months I was completely out of my depth and was sitting across from the general manager wondering if I was still going to be employed after this meeting. That was the first moment I truly realised that as a company Michael Hill did keep their promises, and were actually committed to training and nurturing talent.

Mike Parsell offered me a lifeline: go and retrain, and try again. What he probably didn't know was that he had just taught me the very best lesson of my working life to date: it is okay to make mistakes, no matter how large, provided that you ask for help and learn from the mistakes you have made.

I spent the next six years managing stores before moving into the human resources department. Once again I had to learn how to succeed. I started as a trainer and then became a human resources advisor. In 2004 I saw an opportunity. The company didn't have a training manager, so I took a chance and submitted a proposal. A week later I had a new role as the training and communications manager.

Today I am one of the senior management team, working with the CEO, the board and Michael Hill. I work with amazing people. I make decisions and shape strategies that affect thousands of people, and, best of all, I have been able to play a part in building a truly successful international company.

Michael Hill has taught me that you have to make your own opportunities, you have to continue to learn and strive to improve yourself, and you can't sit still waiting for something to happen. You have to put your hand in the air, have a go, and with hard work and determination you will achieve your goals.

Life truly is what you make it — and what the past 15 years have taught me is this: never stop learning, and never stop striving to achieve.

Opportunity is missed by most
people because it is dressed in
overalls and looks like work.
Thomas A Edison

Chapter 7

WORK IS THE WRONG WORD

That's right — I think there's been a mistake somewhere. Work is the wrong word for what we all do every day. It should be called 'fun'. And there is absolutely no reason why that can't be the reality.

There are two approaches that I believe are essential to finding satisfaction in work, and therefore in life. The first is to find something you enjoy, and do it. Don't just do it as a hobby. Make it your life. The more you do it, the better you'll become, and the more you'll enjoy yourself.

In his recent book, *Outliers*, the American economist Malcolm Gladwell wrote that truly high achievers are not created by birth, upbringing or education, but by pure dedication. He examined the lives of highly successful individuals and found a common theme: they had all put massive amounts of time and effort into their chosen crafts. The Beatles, for example, enjoyed making music so much that they spent years and years perfecting their technique. They went to Germany and played for years in clubs and bars — long before they ever became famous in Britain, or entered the charts.

Gladwell estimated it takes up to 10,000 hours for any individual to perfect a skill. If you're working a 40-hour week, that's nearly five years of solid concentration. So it naturally follows that if you're going to devote years of your life to something, it had better be something you enjoy.

For me, it was sales. Once I began my apprenticeship with my father at Fishers in Whangarei, I learned all about the art of being a good salesperson: detailed knowledge of products and markets; the ability to project genuine warmth and interest; the judgement to gauge when a customer is teetering on the edge of a sale, and how to gently push the purchase through to conclusion; the observation skills to read body language; the patience to listen carefully and pick up clues about what someone might be looking for in a casual conversation; and the care and dedication to making sure stock is attractively presented and sparkling clean at all times.

I spent 23 years of my life learning all of this — probably too long. I was hamstrung by fear, doubted my own abilities and was intimidated by my uncle's refusal to pass the business on to me. But the point is that by the time I finally made my move, I was ready. I knew what I was doing. My apprenticeship had encompassed not only perfecting the art of sales, but also learning in detail how to run a business efficiently, manage staff, deal with buyers and understand all the countless transactions and interactions that go into making a retail operation.

And the reason I was able to remain working in my uncle's shop for so long was that I really, truly loved sales. I got a huge kick out of every sale I made. And Christine and I both adored the creative process that went along with our involvement, such as designing the window displays. It was enormous fun, just like selling jewellery was fun.

And that's another clue as to why our business worked on a larger scale, when we finally set up on our own as Michael Hill Jeweller and began taking on the world. We didn't treat it as just a straight retail operation, like selling sausages or screwdrivers or reams of paper. We made it a fun, creative, inventive business. Right from the beginning, it was a business of ideas. We wanted to keep the thrills coming, every day — and we knew that if we were excited and energised by the look of our shops, and the window displays, and the beautiful stock, then our customers and staff would be, too.

And guess what? It worked.

And all along, we were looking for a new thrill. Next was our second store, in Hastings, on the eastern side of the North Island; and all the excitement of creation came again. Before we knew it, we were opening a third store, then dreaming of having seven stores in seven years. In another eye-blink the dream had grown to 1000 stores in 20 years; our dream expanding with every success. The very process of creating something was a joy in itself.

It's crazy to underestimate the joy that can be derived from creativity. Both Christine and I have always enjoyed the process of creation more than the concrete result of that process. In other words, we get more of a kick out of coming up with ideas — like designing a boat, drawing plans and thinking about furnishings and decks and cabins and portholes — than we do from actually sitting on the deck of our finished boat holding a cocktail.

I think that spirit of creativity might be what has always pushed us to keep looking for new challenges for ourselves. Don't get me wrong — we're not so foolish as to sit around moaning to one another about how annoying it is that our boat is finished. It's just that we get a huge thrill from inventing and designing and imagining, so we're always searching for a new field of dreams.

Christine in the late fifties, unpacking the kiln at art college.

It's the same with Christine's practice as a visual artist. She has always made artworks, and was in fact an art teacher when I met her in Whangarei. For her, making art is not about the ego boost of 'being an artist', or even about selling her pieces — even though her creations are sought after by collectors. It's just the pure love of creating something. She finds the whole business of staging an opening and selling a collection a bit tedious, to be honest; she'd rather be back in her studio, painting something new.

Here's my second point: make the most of the talents you have. Make sure you do what you love, and love what you do.

If you sit on a morning train or bus, how often do you see

city workers looking as if they're on their way to their own execution? It's become a cliché that work is drudgery, boredom, something we just need to get through and survive so we can leave at the end of the day and do what we really like.

What a sad situation. There's a message I try to get through to all the people in our company, around the world: get involved. Take an interest. If the shop is looking scruffy, or the production process is clunky and old-fashioned, or there's a glaring problem in the way the company works, why not try to fix it? Make the effort to think about how things could be different. Raise the problem with your manager. And if you are the manager, make sure your staff are trusting and confident enough to feel they can raise issues with you and know that they'll be heard.

I understand that for many people life seems a grind: get a job, start a family, buy a house and stay there. What's wrong with that? Nothing. And if you are happy and satisfied and fulfilled then, well, you're probably not reading this book. If you are ready to strive for more though, now is the time to get started.

There I was, virtually the village idiot, plodding happily away but dreaming of more and waiting until the ripe old age of 40 to do something about it. But I *did* do something, and I found out how much more fulfilling life could be.

And the great thing is, it's never too late for the fun to start.

Having fun at an early managers' conference, 1986.

Michael Hill staff story: Sue Szylvester
Group advertising manager

I left school at the age of 15 and went to live in London, where I worked my way through a number of jobs from dental nurse to personal assistant. I married at 17 and had three children by the age of 24. I was now a housewife, working on the second chapter of my life.

By the time the children were at school, I was ready for work again. I managed to train myself on a friend's computer and got a job as a personal assistant working in the transport industry. I worked in transport for almost 10 years, from small trucking companies to international freight-forwarding. With my amazing time-management and organisational skills, I was invincible and soon on my way to the top . . .

I was working as a temporary assistant in the minister's department for transport when I was approached by a recruitment officer who asked me if I would like to work with jewellery. I thought to myself, Who wouldn't?

Then the phone call came, asking me to come back in for another chat. I wondered what else I could tell them. But the chat was to let me know that I had the position, my dream job in a jewellery company, Michael Hill Jeweller.

I soon realised three things: that I wanted to be more than just a personal assistant; that this was a very exciting company; and that there were lots of opportunities. Back then, we didn't have an advertising department and I thought I could set it up and run it in Australia. This was my first goal and I learned as much as I could from the managing director Mike Parsell, while doing my job. I listened intently and asked a lot of questions. Three years later Mike handed over the reins and I finally had my own department, running the advertising for Australia.

In May 2003 the company was beginning to change rapidly. Mike had taken over as CEO of the company and the decision was made to have one head office in Australia. So I was asked to take over the advertising for New Zealand too — a big challenge, but a very exciting market to learn about and understand.

I'm now the group advertising manager and we're growing at a rapid rate. In September 2008 we launched into the US with the acquisition of 17 stores in greater Chicago, which means we now have 250 stores in four countries. Our company goal is to have 1000 stores by 2022.

For someone who didn't even finish high school and has no formal qualifications, it's amazing to look back on everything I have achieved. At Michael Hill, the opportunities are boundless. I truly believe that if you work hard and set goals, the sky is the limit!

Michael Hill staff story: Patrick Sauter
Regional manager, Victoria

I started at Michael Hill Jeweller as a part-time sales professional and at the time I simply saw it as just another temporary part-time job in a long line of such jobs (mostly labouring positions) I had held to help support myself through university and the student flatting lifestyle! However, I was incredibly money hungry and when I finished my degree I soon became aware of the financial opportunities that Michael Hill offered over other employers. I was also aware of an environment in which your personal efforts and results were extremely measurable, and transparent for everyone to see, and to which career progression was directly linked.

So, the moment I finished my degree I set my mind to moving from a sales professional to store-manager role. Seven months later I moved from Hamilton to Auckland and was appointed as a sales manager of the largest store in the Michael Hill group, and five months after that I was appointed as store manager in Browns Bay, Auckland — the first store of my own. For the next three years I worked with only two goals in mind: to make as much money as I possibly could (through the generous store-manager bonus scheme) and to earn the manager's role at the Manukau store, the largest in the group, where I had started as a sales manager.

Eventually, I got my second wish. I was where I had always wanted to be — running the store I had always wanted, and making more money than I had ever conceived possible. Although I have been tempted away from the company several times over the years, I am yet to find a company where results, recognition and reward are so closely linked. The hours were also extremely long, but no one demanded them of you other than yourself, out of drive and determination to win in an environment that made it feel worthwhile. Previously I had always been, or at least thought I had been, motivated by money, but on reflection it has always been my own need to win, in an organisation that promotes an extremely competitive spirit.

I have since left store-management roles and am now enjoying a broader strategic influence as a regional manager in Victoria, Australia, which has provided new challenges and rewards, as well as a clearer vision of where I would like my career to go in the future.

My eight years at Michael Hill have had a 'work hard, play hard' theme, with many hard-fought wins and successes, and countless social events that have taken years off the lives of everyone involved! I continue to look forward to any challenges we might face as a business and to overcoming each one of them in my current role and the next.

Michael Hill staff story: Tom Lima
Construction and projects manager

In 1993 I was immigrating to Australia from America. My wife Jay saw an advertisement in the paper for store managers for a jewellery company, and she thought it seemed a perfect fit for me. How right she was!

I had a group interview with about 50 people in one room. I listened to managers talk of how Michael Hill gave them the opportunity to run a business as if it were their own, but with one big positive: they didn't have to pay for it. It was at that point that I felt like a round peg in a round hole.

Very soon, I not only had to learn the Michael Hill thing, but I also had to learn the Australian thing. I questioned everything and learned the operations that would be needed to run a Michael Hill business. My fun in Surfers Paradise only lasted 6 months, 9 days and 16 hours before I was offered my first store.

Castle Towers, Sydney was trading as the worst store in the group. I soon realised that this store was an absolute gold mine that was ready to rock. Within three months, I had the staff and operations sorted out. It was then that the store started to go off! Castle Towers gave me the understanding of how to turn a business around from red dots to gold stars.

It was almost a year to the day when I received a phone call from Mike Parsell asking if I was interested in moving back to Brisbane to run the flagship store. On the first day of my six-year tender at the Myer Centre I realised that all my life experiences and all my education could not have prepared me for this store. Some days I felt that I was winning while other days the store had the upper hand. The Myer Centre sharpened my multi-tasking skills.

In 2000 Michael Hill gave me the opportunity to venture into the operational branch of the business. A 12-month contract as a project coordinator became my next adventure. The main duty of this role was to spearhead the expansion of the Super Stores in Australia. Mike then handed over to me all the new stores and refits within Australia. This job gave me the ability to create programmes, develop operational systems and expand my knowledge of project management. I was self-driven to the point of obsession. Striving to create the perfect new store opening was my goal. Building systems that would increase my span of control was a skill that Mike inadvertently passed on to me, and I can only now realise its power.

With the closure of the New Zealand head office, a new opportunity presented itself: to run the construction operation in the two countries. I quickly realised that the only difference between running the New Zealand construction and the Australian construction was a bit of a language thing and a three-hour flight. The story was the same in both countries: 'get plans, design shops, build shops and open shops'.

In 2005 Canada was added to the list and in 2008 the US was included as well. My 16-year journey with Michael Hill has been very exciting. Knowing the answers before the questions are asked has been my secret weapon.

When people talk, listen completely.
Most people never listen.
Ernest Hemingway

Chapter 8

KEEP AN EYE ON THE
UNDERDOG

So much of business is about mental fitness and awareness. No matter how good your idea is, and no matter how perfect all the conditions are for you to succeed, it is perfectly possible to undermine yourself and your business with clouded thinking. A lack of confidence in yourself, an inaccurate reading of the people around you, or lapsing into the lazy mental habit of always expecting success can all be disastrous.

I've observed over the years that the people who seem, on the surface, most likely to succeed are often the ones who end up struggling — and, conversely, the people who are quiet, retiring, or diffident in their early years are often the greatest success stories. The most brilliant schoolkids aren't necessarily going to grow up to be the highest achievers; in fact, I've noticed the opposite is often true.

Why is that the case? I think it's because the experience of struggle and difficulty are far more valuable than the experience of success. It's not just about people who have everything handed to them on a silver platter by their parents; I've seen several naturally bright and incisive children, who work hard at school and get high marks purely as a result of their own work, falter once they leave school. It's not because they don't know how to work — it's just that they haven't tasted the bitterness of defeat.

Simply put, a bit of struggle is good for you — especially when you're creating a business, and especially when you're living through tough economic times, as we are now.

This links to my belief about the power of mistakes; it's important not to fear errors or mis-steps, because they have a twin purpose of teaching you hard lessons and making you leaner and stronger. In just the same way, it can be hugely beneficial to the business mind to understand the feeling of hardship, both at an intellectual and a visceral level.

Literature is full of characters who, upon being told 'you can't do that', turn around and conquer the world. It's also a common theme among successful businesspeople; many will have an experience of rejection and dejection that has spurred them to achieve.

My own personal story is a good example.

'You might as well get used to the fact,' intoned Jack Glanville, my maths master at Whangarei Boys' High, one awful day, 'that boy will never amount to much in life.'

Mr Glanville was speaking to my parents, and had come around to the house especially to tell them that I was a lost cause.

I was 13 years old. I had always struggled with school; although I was intelligent, I was not academic in a traditional sense. I was also terribly shy and lonely. By the first year of high school, I had begun to think I might like to be an architect when I grew up; I loved drawing and painting, and had a particular interest in buildings and design.

'But your maths is so poor,' said everyone from my teachers to my parents. 'You'll never make it as an architect.' The consensus was that I shouldn't even waste my time attempting to study architecture. I was struggling so much with maths that my parents were paying for extra coaching from Mr Glanville, but I wasn't giving him much joy. To his immense frustration, I remained firmly at the bottom of the maths class.

So when he came to visit my parents, the news was all bad. 'Not only is his maths abysmal,' he announced to my parents, 'but his English is atrocious as well.' As far as Jack was concerned, I was besmirching his reputation as a tutor by remaining the worst pupil.

Billie burst into tears, while I sat there staring at Mr Glanville. I couldn't believe he was writing me off so comprehensively. My father became quite agitated. 'That's ridiculous,' he sputtered. 'Of course he will amount to something.'

Jack Glanville shook his head, plainly frustrated that the father was apparently as blind as the useless son. 'Just give him a trade and don't put too much pressure on him, or you'll destroy him,' he said. 'The school has been trying to make the best of him, but it all just fizzles out. He's impossible to teach.'

Mr Glanville's attitude was reflected by the school authorities, who moved me into the trade stream. I began woodwork and metalwork classes, at which I proceeded to excel at even less than I had at maths and English. Nobody seemed to notice that I was good at playing the violin and loved art. The things I was good at seemed to count for nothing.

I don't want all this to sound too Dickensian. I wasn't beaten or kept in the coal cellar. The point is simply this: I was widely regarded as a dud, and nobody hesitated to let me know. And I don't regret that experience. I heard Jack Glanville's words ringing in my ears for many, many years afterwards. I still remember them with clarity — and I remember how they made me feel. As I later discovered, I did have hidden strengths — but they didn't emerge fully until I'd spent 23 years working for my uncle and feeling pretty unfulfilled in my business life.

Being told I couldn't do something — just as I was later thwarted and blocked by my uncle — made me even more determined to do it. And that's why I feel the way I do about mistakes and hardships in a business — and about difficult financial times. Although it might not feel this way at the time, challenges really do make you stronger, leaner, better. They're not to be feared. They are to be embraced.

It's funny — our business is always the underdog, in some ways. Over the years, we've become the leading jewellery brand in our major markets. In Australia and New Zealand when young couples get engaged, it's often a natural choice to come to Michael Hill Jeweller to select a ring. We're a big employer, a big buyer, a big presence in the business scene.

That's a nice status. But we haven't allowed that to become our only status — we have kept expanding into markets where we are unfamiliar; where people haven't a clue who or what Michael Hill is, and couldn't care less. That means every time we make a big move, we are the underdog again — the unknown brand that has to prove itself.

This might sound like a tedious, repetitive pattern — but

actually I think it is a critical part of our success story. We're always fresh. We're always hungry. And every new market we have entered has made us leaner and more efficient. Every time we enter a new market we learn a great deal. Sticking your neck out can be costly, but you can't put a price on the value it adds to the core brand. Opening stores in Australia strengthened the New Zealand side of the business and the same has happened since we opened in Canada. Every one of these markets has a different set of values, a different culture, different tastes and we glean innumerable different ways of retailing in these markets that can often be insightful lessons elsewhere.

Let me give you an example.

When we moved to Canada, things were really tough. We pulled our usual trick of a huge opening sale, discounting all the old stock from the previous owners at ridiculous prices. It sold reasonably well — perhaps not as well as in New Zealand or Australia, but well enough. But we couldn't afford television advertising, which in Canada at the time was perilously expensive, and there were so many channels that we barely knew where to begin. Instead, we distributed catalogues by the tens of thousands. The catalogues worked quite well: people came to the sales and after that would come into the stores and look, but still they would not buy.

The truth was, they didn't like our stock. We had brought our jewellery over from Australia, assuming Canadians would buy it because we had a broader range of designs than other local retailers and because we had what we considered a bit of European flair.

But the Canadians didn't like it. The market was a lot more conservative, it seemed. The women might browse but seemed hesitant to buy for themselves. Also, as the new people on the block, we just hadn't earned their trust.

My daughter Emma, who was running the Canadian business, would be on the phone to me saying: 'They just won't buy. I can get them in the shop but I can't close the sale.'

This came as quite a shock; Emma is a great salesperson, family or not. If she couldn't sell our diamonds in Canada, nobody could. So, we realised that something had to change and started analysing exactly what it was the customers didn't want.

It turned out that our rings were all wrong for a start: Canadians liked white gold and we had yellow; they liked four-claw settings and we had eight. Most importantly, though, they liked a different grade of diamonds. The other Canadian jewellery shops were selling white diamonds that were included, or flawed, whereas we sold a higher quality diamond that was much cleaner and brighter but double the price of the flawed ones, which made them hard to sell. The Canadians thought that bigger was better and would rather have a one-carat diamond that was more included than a near flawless one that was half the size.

Well, you can fight that for a while but it's a losing battle. If anyone was going to change, it was unlikely to be the wider Canadian public.

So we altered a lot of Australian stock and started buying locally. Gradually, it began to work. What's more, we realised that if this worked in Canada, it might work in Australia and New Zealand too; so we brought those diamonds over to our other markets.

The outcome? They sell like crazy as they are almost half the price! The customer, as you know, is always right.

So, being the Canadian underdog made us a better, stronger business both in that market and, by extension, elsewhere in the world. We're going through it again right now in the United States — building the brand, learning what customers like and loathe.

I sometimes think of it as a bit like being an Olympic-level swimmer. Churning up and down the lanes in your home pool is great — and it's necessary to do plenty of kilometres to get fit — but you'll never improve much if you don't race against the best. Diving into a strange pool, filled with swimmers who push and challenge you, is the only way to really get faster — and ultimately, hopefully, become the champion.

Little boy lost

Nobody ever called me Richard, not even once. Officially, it was my name — Richard Michael Hill, born December 1938 — but from my first moments, I was Michael. In our rather odd family, that sort of thing was normal. My mother Billie's name was actually Hilda, and my father was christened Albert, but always known as Dickie.

I was a timid little fellow. My mother loved to show me off, and so I was like Little Lord Fauntleroy: always impeccably dressed in the elaborate outfits she made for me; my hair always smooth and well combed:;my clothes too neatly pressed for a normal Kiwi boy. I was never allowed to get dirty. I never seemed to fit in with other children.

I was like Little Lord Fauntleroy: always impeccably dressed in elaborate outfits.

Clockwise, from top left: Me, salesman at Fishers the Jewellers, 1960; as a young boy with Dickie and Billie, 1950; home was 28 Manse Street, Whangarei. My mother never liked that house; Christine, in a crocheted dress she had made, me, Auntie June, Uncle Arthur Fisher, Billie and Dickie, 1969.

Starting primary school was a torment. I seriously did not want to go, and for months lived in dread of my first day, staring balefully at the school from our front gate. As Billie walked me down the road on that first morning, I bawled like hell, and didn't stop until she came and picked me up at the end of the day. The headmistress, Miss Lupton, was a kind woman, and I eventually grew to quite enjoy school. I stopped crying, at any rate. Although I was shy, I liked reading, writing and numbers, as maths was then known.

But by the age of 11, I was starting to lose my enthusiasm. As I moved into intermediate school, I felt more and more that I really didn't fit in. I felt all wrong at school. I was good at marbles, which had proved quite helpful at primary school, but at intermediate this didn't count for much.

Things weren't great at home, either. Even as a small child I remember being aware of the strain in our Manse Street house. Billie was not really satisfied with life. She didn't particularly like our home, which my parents had built together. 'It looks like a state house,' she'd tell my father. She was also deeply frustrated with their work situation.

I believe my parents weren't really compatible. She was careful with money; he didn't care whether he had it or not. He had no trouble making it, and no trouble spending it, either. They were destined for a life of arguments and walkouts and dramatic returns, passion and pride. And into the middle of all that emotion, I was born.

Like many only children, I led a lonely existence. I was much treasured, much indulged, much mollycoddled, much insulated and much shown off. I don't doubt for a moment my parents loved me but they didn't seem to know what to do with the introverted, unusual child they had brought into the world.

To make things worse, life outside the home was also hard. Uncle Arthur's wife, Jenny, had died in her 40s after a local doctor gave her gold injections as a treatment for arthritis. The use of gold injections has since been refined, and is still used for arthritis, but

Billie and Dickie, when I was very young, circa 1936.

Dickie and Bob Johnson at their weekly singalong on Radio Northland, 1958.

in those days it was still an experimental therapy and the doctor gave Jenny an accidental overdose. She never recovered. Arthur was left to raise their seven-year-old daughter Jean alone. My mother, Billie, stepped in to help care for Jean, and she became the closest thing I had to a sister.

During the polio epidemic of 1945, we became especially close. Mum, Jean and I all moved to Arthur's beach house at McLeod Bay, Whangarei Heads, while the men remained in town running the shop. Billie taught us by correspondence and would take us in Arthur's heavy dinghy to catch snapper and gurnard in the bay. I loved fishing, but I hated coming home at dusk. I was terrified of the rats in the boatshed. I was terrified, indeed, of many things.

All of New Zealand, and especially Whangarei, is pas-sionate about sport. I wasn't. Thanks to Dickie, I was interested in music. I had grown up to the sound of him playing his treasured grand piano, and he gave me lessons. Even Billie would stop her baking and sewing to smile while she watched us playing together — so I grew to equate music with happy times.

Sport, however, was not my forte. I could not even execute a forward roll without going sideways or backwards. I was small, I was nervous, I was not really interested. Not a good combination in a sport-focused school, in an outdoorsy city, in a rugby-saturated country.

Strangely, I was quite keen on golf, which probably didn't endear me to the other boys busy playing cricket and rugby. When I was about 11 or 12, I created a little golf course at our house. I mowed circles for greens and put upside down baked bean cans in the ground for the holes. I remember having prizes to give to the neighbourhood kids who played on my golf course but, generally, friends were not a big part of my later school years.

Michael Hill, aged six.

I suppose small, clean, impeccably dressed boys who like music and golf will always be a target for bullying, so it's probably no surprise that at high school I had become an easy target for the bigger, sportier boys. The teachers didn't seem to notice. If they were aware, they certainly didn't do anything about it. They probably thought I needed toughening up. I got the cane a few times, probably for not doing homework, but I didn't mind that. It was nothing compared to the punishment being meted out by the school bullies. They would wait for me at lunchtime and after school, and punch and kick me.

On occasion, I tried to fight back — but I had limited physical strength and no allies. Attempting to defend myself only seemed to enrage the bullies more, and the intensity of their dislike only increased. My learning ability was affected. I was so worried about what the kids were going to do to me after the lessons ended that

I didn't listen to the teachers. I couldn't concentrate. I would sit there feeling nauseous, watching the clock's hands tick towards the end of class. That made me even more miserable: not only was I lonely and afraid, I was getting poor marks.

I never told a soul about the bullying, not even my mum. When I look back now, I feel so sad for the isolated little boy I was — especially after having children and grandchildren of my own and seeing how much fun life can be with siblings. I was living in a cloud, a horribly lonely cloud. I looked wrong. I didn't play sport well. I was embarrassingly neat. I was flunking all my classes except science and art. So why didn't I do anything about it? Why didn't I complain?

I just couldn't imagine how anyone could help me.

The sound of music

Sitting by myself in the sunshine at school one day, I heard the most amazing sound I'd ever experienced — the notes of a violin, floating out across the playground. I stood up and listened for the source of this wonderful music. It was a prefabricated building that served as the music classroom, and inside was the music teacher, Peter Green, playing his violin. I went in and stood for a while, listening to him playing, and we started talking. From that moment, I was determined to learn to play this magical instrument. It seemed so fluid and easy — all Peter's concentration was focused on his fingering hand, while the bow swept back and forth across the strings with seemingly no effort at all.

I went straight home and begged my parents to let me learn to play — but they were decidedly reluctant. I'd been learning the piano for years, and both Dickie and Billie thought I should continue. 'But the piano's so difficult,' I moaned. 'Please, please, let me play the violin.'

Eventually, my pestering paid off, and they bought me a new violin from Haslett's Music Store in Cameron Street. I think my parents could see I was unhappy, and needed something I could be good at. It was true: I felt I was pretty useless at life generally, but from the first moment I picked up my violin, I felt I'd found something that suited me perfectly.

My ear was very good, which helped, but Peter Green was the catalyst for a complete change in my life. His natural enthusiasm and drive made my progress with the violin smooth. I studied under a couple of different teachers, and joined the school orchestra, all with Peter's encouragement. He got the two Whangarei schools — the boys' and girls' high schools — together at one stage and created a concert using the orchestra and a big choir that filled the whole town hall and I was part of it.

For the first time, I really felt like I fitted in — and the passion just grew. As I neared the end of school, I was having violin lessons with a Danish music teacher, Agee Neilsen, who had come to Whangarei. He had played in the Danish National Orchestra and was an accomplished musician with a passion for teaching — a brilliant combination. Much as I loved Peter Green, once I started playing with Agee even I could tell I was vastly improving.

It was a great feeling. I'd never shown much aptitude for anything, so to suddenly be considered able — even talented — was an unfamiliar, but definitely pleasant, sensation. Then he suggested I make the violin my career. I was ecstatic — recognition at last, and a future. Brilliant.

Billie and Dickie, not surprisingly, were horrified when I came home and announced: 'I'm going to be a professional violinist.' To their credit, however, they got behind me. I really appreciate the enthusiasm they showed me; it was a fairly unusual ambition for a boy from a modest Whangarei home. Dad bought me a Gand & Bernadel violin, a French antique, which must have cost him a packet. I can only hope I appeared sufficiently grateful, although I suspect that, like most teenagers, I simply seized it and rushed off to my room to play without a word.

Music brought a new discipline to my life. I left school at 16,

My parents, not surprisingly, were horrified at first when I came home and announced: 'I'm going to be a professional violinist.'

and every morning I would start my day with a run or brisk walk. I weighed around nine stone, and would probably have blown away in a brisk southerly, but I was keen to keep fit. My violin practice would start at nine and I would go through till midday, in my bedroom, then have a bit of a break and start again at one, going through till four or five.

Twice a week I would go for lessons with my teacher on the other side of town, and spend the day practising in one of the rooms of his house. As I whizzed up and down the scales and advanced to sonatas and concerto pieces, I could hear the beginners' violins wheezing and sawing in other rooms of the house — a little distracting, but a good reminder of how far I'd come. I didn't find it hard work. I enjoyed every moment of the year I spent studying the violin full-time.

Dickie was quite proud of me, I think, but a lot of other people, including Uncle Arthur, thought I was a fruit-loop. I can't really blame Arthur, I suppose — he was a conservative man running a busy shop, and his weedy nephew was spending all his days secreted in a room playing the fiddle. It must have seemed very odd.

During that year I competed in a violin concerto competition run by the *New Zealand Herald*. The experience of playing before a live audience thrilled me, but I was disappointed to only come fourth. Far from being deterred, I came home and practised even harder. My sliver of self-confidence was boosted, too, by attending a music school in Cambridge, in the Waikato, where there was not only an orchestra to play in and other violinists to play with, there were girls. Astonishingly, none of my fellow musicians seemed to care that I couldn't play sport. They were friendly and open. In this musical crowd, I actually made friends — I was surrounded by people who didn't think I was odd in the slightest.

The National Orchestra — which travelled around the country in those days — came to town and we all went to see its evening performance in the Whangarei Town Hall. Unbeknownst to me, my parents had spoken with the lead violinist and arranged an audition for me, to see if I had the potential to get into the orchestra.

'Come on, Michael,' my father announced the morning after the concert, 'we've got a surprise for you.' Completely unprepared, I rushed down to the town hall, where I played a Handel sonata in front of the violinist, as the rest of the orchestra packed up their instruments around us. They were clunking shut their cases, dimming the lights and scraping seats across the floor as I played — and when I finished, the violinist nodded and turned to my parents.

'Your son has potential,' he said, 'but I'm afraid he started playing too late in life. I can't see him making a career out of this.'

Too late in life? But I had taken up the violin at 11. How could I be too late? It was the Jack Glanville scenario all over again. I was devastated.

My parents took me home, and I spent a couple of days in a daze. I couldn't believe my dreams had been squashed so quickly.

I wandered about the house, feeling utterly lost. And then Uncle Arthur showed up. In his brand new Holden, he pulled up in front of the house one evening and strode inside. After the barest of pleasantries he took me aside, cleared his throat and looked at me with his sternest gaze.

'You've been mucking your parents about too long, fiddling around, wasting your life,' he declared. 'It's time you got a real job, son. You're going to start at Fishers the Jewellers as a watchmaker tomorrow. I want you there at 7.30 sharp.'

Uncle Arthur always called me 'son' but there was nothing paternal about our relationship. I never got the impression Arthur liked me. And he was about to like me a whole lot less, for a whole lot longer.

When Uncle Arthur came around that night and ordered me to start working in the shop, my parents didn't say much. I knew, however, they were in cahoots with him. They might not have been brave enough to reshape my life on their own, but they firmly believed there was no future for me in music. They were probably right. To be a top solo artist you need exceptional talent and total dedication. Every day must be spent practising — and only a very few reach the top. Back then, I didn't know that. I just knew the music was gone.

My self-esteem was at a new low.

Imagination is more
important than knowledge.
Albert Einstein

Chapter 9

NOW YOU SEE IT: THE POWER OF VISUALISATION

Now is a very good time. I don't just mean for me — although it's true that I'm happy, healthy and as excited by my life as ever. I mean that if you have a goal in life, now is the perfect time to start achieving it. But for all of us, deciding upon a goal is one of the hardest parts of the struggle.

You might wonder: Who does this fellow think he is? What right has he to bang on about opportunity and lament those who don't have as much luck as him? I'm nobody special, really. I have nothing special. But I see people like my late father, who I don't believe ever achieved a fraction of what he could have, or the girl down the road too scared to start her business, or the old codger in town who waited his whole working life to retire but did nothing to prepare for it, and I think, What a waste.

We are all capable of shining — once you've experienced the feeling of doing well at something, you become a zealot. You want to keep shining on, and you want everyone else to shine as well.

People have asked me why I didn't just give up after the first wave of success. I was a successful businessman, I was making plenty of money, and I was enjoying my family life. But here's a secret: it's actually easier to keep going than it is to stop. Once you begin achieving your dreams, it's such an incredible buzz that you won't want to stop — and you'll be surrounded by people whom you need to motivate and encourage. If you have a dream, it's much easier to do that.

But how do you get started with success? A slow economy presents the perfect opportunity to take the time and effort to think about your life. What do you want? Where would you like to be in five years, 10 years, 20 years?

I don't want you to think about it while you're cooking dinner, or strap-hanging on a train, or jogging along the waterfront. That's not good enough. These questions are serious, and they deserve truly serious concentration. Set aside a morning, or an entire day if you can. Make it a rainy day — less temptation to head outside. Turn off the television, the radio, the mobile phone and put your laptop to sleep. Write down, on a huge sheet of paper, your dreams. And don't stint on the ambition. There's no point writing: 'Improve writing skills' or 'Look into how hard it would be to run a coffee shop', or 'Lose weight'. You need to think big — and be specific.

Remember, you're not attempting to visualise a slightly improved version of yourself — you're conjuring up the best, brightest, boldest person you can possibly be. So how about: 'Write a novel and get it published', or 'Open my own café within a year', or 'Fit into a size-12 dress.'

Those are the kind of focused, clear goals that will really inspire you, every day — and they will carry you forward. It doesn't matter what area you want to achieve in: a weight-loss goal is just as valid as a desire to be CEO of a finance conglomerate.

The reason I'm so adamant about focused goals is that I've seen too many people set goals they have little or no intention of achieving. You've seen it too — in fact, I'd be willing to bet you've set a few goals that were later conveniently forgotten. They're called New Year's resolutions — and the reason they've become a longstanding joke is that most resolutions are entirely vague and waffly. It's very easy to wriggle out of a goal like 'eat less chocolate' or 'start my own business' — they're not specific, they're not realistic and they're easy to forget. If you have a deadline and a concrete goal, it will be almost impossible for you to wriggle out of your obligation to do something about it.

All you need to do is know what you want. Give yourself enough quiet time and you'll find out exactly what that is. It might be developing a new kind of medicine, or creating a happier family life.

Start by cutting out the negative thoughts that creep into your mind; the little voice that says: 'It's too hard. You're too late. Forget about it.' Negativity is a killer of dreams. Don't listen to people who try to demean your dreams. If friends and relatives are perpetually negative about your goal, don't bother discussing it with them any more. Instead, find people who are prepared to support you, and focus on talking to them. The most harmful negativity comes from within — but there is one effective way I know to quiet your own internal doubt and fear: visualise.

I don't mean that in some namby-pamby esoteric way. I mean actually picturing what you want in your mind. Sit quietly and imagine yourself driving the car you want, or opening your tenth branch office — whatever you want. Images are enormously powerful in our cognitive processing. I have discovered that if I can find a picture of what I want and place it just inside my diary, or have it come up as wallpaper on my computer screen, I'm constantly reminded of my goal.

It has taken me a long time to work out the kind of goal-setting that works for me. I've tried writing a list of my dreams and sticking it up on the wall. I've tried creating a series of mini-targets and deadlines, and putting them in my diary so I can feel the idea progressing. But I've found this sort of thing too pedantic and boring to sustain my interest.

Just keep it simple. And it is a ridiculously simple discipline.

I pictured my first shop, with my name up the top, the small windows and wide doorway, long before it existed. When I had that shop, I pictured six more. And as our business grew, I pictured more shops, and more, and more. I saw our business expanding overseas. I pictured the things I wanted — a boat, a new home — and they happened.

It takes time to draw up these mental visuals but I practise and practise and practise until the picture is so clear in my mind that it's as though what I am imagining already physically exists and this makes doubting it redundant. It's there already.

It's extraordinary how powerful an image can be. It's part determination, part inspiration and a little bit of magic, I believe. I have been constantly astounded by how I've been able to achieve all the things I've pictured in this way.

In 1981, when we had three stores, I began thinking about

where I wanted the business to go during the next decade.

'Why not seven stores in seven years?' I said to myself one day.

Having come up with the idea, I set about convincing my team it could be achieved. In doing this, I learned another of the big lessons of my business life: having a vision is the path to inspiring your team.

If your staff members know there is an overriding goal or vision to work towards, they will naturally be imbued with a greater sense of purpose. Instead of showing up at work and just getting through another day, they are gradually building up to a more interesting future.

The vision of seven shops in seven years also emphasised the importance of delegation: I knew if I was going to keep opening shops and still have time to spend with Christine and the children, I needed to share the load. I needed people who were willing to

Top: Andy Rout and Mary Muir, who left Fishers to join me, standing outside our first store site in Whangarei, 1979.
Bottom: The pet shop that was destined to become our Palmerston North store.

learn the art of retail, and who could cover my weaknesses. That meant, in particular, finding people who were good with accounts. I still had no clue about maths — I was a salesman, and my talent was building rapport and attracting attention. There was no point pretending I was a numbers genius, so instead, I hired fresh talent who already knew what they were doing. That helped me create the foundations of the brilliant team I have today. They've all helped me achieved that goal, and all the goals I have set in the years since.

By 1986 I had the seven shops I'd dreamed of, so it was time to adjust the dream. By the way — this is another key part of my system. As soon as you have achieved your dream, it's time to get out another piece of paper and write down a new set of dreams, formulating a mental picture to help keep the goal clear in your mind.

This time, the horizons would be much bigger.

Together with my board members, I started thinking about what we might be able to do next. At this time, we were a successful New Zealand company. We knew there might be more in store for us, but weren't quite sure what.

About that time, Howard Bretherton introduced me to a friend of his, an accountant named Johnny Ryder. Johnny started doing a bit of consulting for us, and kept mentioning an idea he'd come up with.

'Why don't you float the business on the stock exchange?' he asked one day.

I had never given this prospect a thought. The idea of going public just never entered my mind — we were a private concern, and I'd had no experience of public companies whatsoever. But Johnny thought our concept could work on a much bigger scale.

'You could be worth millions if you continue growing this thing — in Australia,' he said. 'But to go offshore, you need money. Lots of it. And the only way to get lots of money is to float the company.'

It all seemed unbelievable. Australia?

Crossing the Tasman was a well-worn path to disaster for many New Zealand companies — Australian cities were notoriously tough, parochial and competitive markets, and New Zealanders were traditionally eaten alive. But it was 1987. Everyone was floating all sorts of things on the New Zealand Stock Exchange. And the thought of such a bold new adventure was irresistible.

We floated the company in May 1987, structuring our offer so I had a 52.5 per cent share, Howard had seven per cent and the public had the rest. It worked. We raised $3 million — which seems nothing today — but in 1987 it was enough to give Australia a real go.

Suddenly, rather than having to look at my bank accounts to see what I was worth, I could see it on the sharemarket board and in the newspaper. My fortune changed daily, along with the fortunes of our company, and the New Zealand sharemarket generally.

I like being a public company — it is a good yardstick to judge your performance by and creates discipline within the team. It also allows employees to obtain shares, which we encouraged by offering staff a discount on the market price. There is nothing like part-ownership to really make an employee

To shops in
7 years.
12/10/88

feel an emotional investment with a company.

Our plans to move into Australia did not exactly meet with widespread enthusiasm.

'Don't do it,' said many a sharebroker. 'It's not an easy market. Best stick to New Zealand.'

Our friends were equally doubtful. 'Isn't Australia a bit risky?' they asked.

Yes, it was, but we never thought about failure. I don't mean that we were hoping not to fail, or that we intended to do everything possible to avoid failure. I mean we just didn't entertain the concept. Part of our certainty was the fact that Christine and I had thought long and hard about what we would achieve next, and I'd come up with a new and even more brash goal. Seven stores in seven years had been easy. Next up: 70 stores in seven years. We were Australia-bound.

Many years after this, I discovered another way to really bring my goals to the front of my mind — and towards realisation. It was meditation, which was introduced to Christine and me by a wonderful friend and neighbour.

After several years in Australia, we moved home to New Zealand and settled in Queenstown, where we met a landscape artist named Peter Beadle. He had a wonderfully calming presence, and when we became friends he told us he achieved this blissful state through transcendental meditation.

Christine decided to explore meditation — and I came along too. We took a three-day transcendental meditation course in Auckland, and learned to relax and repeat a mantra. The point of this is simply to clear the mind of all the chatter, the negative, unnecessary babbling that's constantly in the background of one's consciousness. To me the experience was like erasing a recording on a tape recorder — suddenly, the distracting hum at the edge of my mind was gone.

It was a step in a direction that I did not expect. It clarified my thinking. It's logical, really: we can only think one thought at a time, but we try to think of many things. How often do you catch yourself simultaneously driving, holding a conversation, listening to the radio, reading the map and sending a text message? It's too much — and yet we do it all day long. No wonder we have trouble focusing.

Once you can clear all this away and just be still, you're immediately in the perfect frame of mind to visualise the future. It's effortless. For 20 minutes two times a day, once upon waking and the other before the evening meal, I entered this world of quietness. Now, goal-setting was much easier than it had ever been. For years I had written down my objectives, placed them in a planner, kept a diary. I had read all the books on motivation I could find — but nothing, nothing anchored me more than this simple process of clearing my mind.

As a result of meditation I had a clear vision of my next move. In my mind's eye, I could see our network of stores grow from the several hundred we already had to 1000 shops, around the world. What's more, I knew I wanted to achieve that daunting number within 20 years. And then I set about spreading the word.

The viral power of goal-setting is amazing. As soon as the word was out about our new goal of 1000 stores in 20 years, the attitude of the whole team changed. Everyone could see where we were going and could sense the excitement. Suddenly, a whole world of opportunities was opening up for each of them, too: managing stores, living abroad, and experiencing this crazy journey together.

I wish I'd known all this earlier. I might not have spent nearly a quarter-century working for my uncle if I'd known how stupidly simple it is to create something better for oneself. Back then, I tended to visualise what I didn't want — a total disaster. If it's possible to bring something you want by visualisation, it's equally possible to visualise yourself towards failure.

I remember being asked to morning tea by a smart friend of my mother's. It was Auckland in the 1950s, and I was temporarily working at a big jewellery store, Stewart Dawsons, on the instructions of my uncle, who wanted me to broaden my experience.

When I arrived at the tearooms, I saw there were small screens separating different parts of the room. They immediately struck fear into my heart because of my terrible clumsiness.

Oh shit, I hope I don't trip over one of them, I thought, slightly panicked.

Of course, that is exactly what happened. I tripped over one of the screens and it fell over, taking with it a stand holding a pot plant, spilling onto a table and alerting everyone within a 10-kilometre radius that a klutz had just entered the premises. See what I mean about internal negativity? It's like irritating chatter inside the head: 'You can't do it, you're hopeless, you're about to trip over and humiliate yourself.' With that kind of cluttered thinking, it is no wonder many people allow their dreams to get away from them.

At Michael Hill, there's not a single staff member that doesn't know about our goal to have 1000 shops by 2022. Putting the idea out there, all the way down through the business, makes it happen. How could it otherwise? And how could it not happen now everyone knows that's where we're headed?

Communication is another crucial element of visualisation. Often, people either neglect to tell others about their goals, or are too shy and afraid to do it. This fear of mistakes is nonsense. We've made colossal mistakes and out of every single one we have emerged wiser and stronger.

All you need to do is to believe that it will happen.

Porsche

Here's another example of the power of visualisation.

In the 1980s, when I was still living in Whangarei and doing quite well in business, I decided I'd quite like a Porsche.

I found a picture of a lovely Porsche 911 Carerra, and stuck it in the front of my diary. Every day when I opened up the diary, I'd see the car. I didn't worry about it, or fret about how I'd never be able to afford it; I just let it be there, as something I'd like to achieve.

One day I heard of a factory worker in Auckland who had won a red Porsche 911 Carerra in a raffle but wanted the cash instead. I found his contact details, gave him a call and offered a price $10,000 lower than the price of a brand-new Porsche.

He wouldn't accept. But I didn't give up. It was an opportunity to use a technique that I'd always admired. There was an old violin dealer in Whangarei, from whom my parents had bought me my prized French violin, who used cash to persuade reluctant sellers.

It had always amazed me how he would carry big bundles of cash, ready to buy expensive items he wanted. I never carried cash — so I rang my local bank and told them I was coming in to withdraw $150,000 from my account.

'I want it in 10-dollar notes, please,' I told the teller, who was slightly alarmed.

You wouldn't believe how big a pile of 15,000 10-dollar notes

looks. I was shocked. It just fitted into two large paper rubbish sacks. With Christine's help, I carried these two huge bags to our car, and we drove to Auckland.

'Mate, I'm here to make you an offer you can't refuse,' I told the factory worker. He looked slightly sceptical — and then I slowly emptied out the two bags of cash onto the large table between us. He vanished behind the pile of money, and I struggled to keep a straight face.

'I'll take it,' he said.

It was a crazy stunt — and I've never tried it again, mainly because it's terribly risky to travel with huge piles of cash — but it worked a treat.

I had my red Porsche — a dream come true.

Four people in a
conference can kill
any idea — no matter
how good it is.
Gene Moore

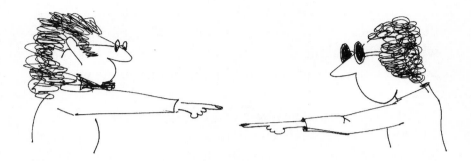

Chapter 10
IT'S NOTHING PERSONAL ...

It ain't what you know, it's who you know.

That's how the saying goes: I'd like to think it's not true — and I believe that to run a successful business, you have to make sure it's not your reality. Sadly, business and sentiment just don't mix. That applies on a whole lot of levels: family, friends, cherished business practices, products you particularly love. As soon as you allow emotion to cloud your cool business judgement, you're in trouble.

Right now is the worst possible time to be sentimental about business. Let's face it, the bank isn't going to be sentimental when it forecloses on your mortgage, or issues a margin call. The creditors aren't going to worry about hurting your feelings when they call in your debts. And the liquidators certainly don't have room for tender moments reminiscing about your entrepreneurial zeal, no matter how nice a person you are.

It can be a hard lesson to learn — and an incredibly difficult one to put into practice — but it's crucial to acquire the habit of switching your mind into clinical business mode when you're making decisions that can affect your livelihood, and the careers and incomes of the people who work for you.

Throughout your business life, people will ask for favours and special treatment. Sometimes they won't ask — but you'll feel obliged to 'do the right thing' by them. And it's crucial to resist that temptation. There was no room for sentimentality, for example, when I first started in my own business. My uncle had refused to sell his business to me, even though common sense would suggest he should have done so. (It would also have been a pretty good business decision on his part, but he was driven more by his dislike of me than by any noble considerations about the business, I fear.)

So I had to learn to play the same game. Setting up in direct competition to a close relative, with every intention of hurting his sales figures, might seem like a brash and tough thing to do. But that was what I felt I had to do. I knew the town. I knew the customers. I certainly knew how the business networks worked — suppliers, deliveries, relations with the council. I could have moved to another town, I guess, and started my business far away from Fishers, saving the awkward situation of competing directly with my uncle. But that wouldn't have been the smartest move — I'd be a stranger in whatever town I went to, starting afresh and throwing away the big advantage I had: local knowledge. So, instead, I turned all those factors to my advantage. I took on my uncle at his own game, on his own turf. And I won.

Part of that came from my personality. I've always loved selling, and the wonderful feeling of succeeding in the difficult task of transferring money from a customer's pocket to the till. In fact, some might say I love it a little too much. I once sold Christine's engagement ring. A lady had come into the store and I'd tried everything in my power to sell her a ring. She wasn't persuaded. Thinking of Dickie's dictum (never give up) I decided to give it one last shot, and invited her into the back room for a cup of tea, to see if anything in our order books appealed.

Christine's amethyst and diamond engagement ring — which I sold.

As it happened, Christine had given me her engagement ring (a big amethyst and diamond cluster) and her watch to clean and polish up.

'That's the ring I want,' the lady exclaimed upon seeing Christine's sparkler sitting on a bench, 'and that's the watch I need, too.'

I sold them.

Before you decide I'm a dreadful husband, you must know that I bought Christine a bigger and more fabulous ring to replace it. In fact, it's a pattern that has continued throughout our lives; I've kept selling her rings and replacing them with even larger ones. I adore Christine with all my heart. But I have sold her engagement ring — the so-called everlasting symbol of my love — over and over again.

Does it seem an odd contradiction? Let me emphasise the point I'm trying to illustrate: sales and sentiment don't mix.

I've had success in business, I am genuinely a friend of the people with whom I work, and I'm blessed with a happy home and family life. But I have always tried to be as tough as possible in my business dealings. That doesn't mean being unethical or underhand: it means being scrupulously honest about what is working, what is failing and what is best for the business. In an enterprise as large as the one Michael Hill International has become, I have a responsibility to my employees and partners to identify and eliminate weaknesses, even when it might be difficult.

Over the years, I have excised parts of the business that haven't worked. When we moved from Fishers to Michael Hill Jeweller, I knew that clocks and antiques had to go, no matter how much we all liked selling them and having them around. I still retained a strong interest in antiques, and eventually they crept back into some of our stores for a while. Unlike the shoes, we were able to make reasonable money out of these items, but the trouble was that they weren't a natural fit in all our stores. In markets where the buyers were predominantly young, or the sales were skewed to the lower end of our range, antiques just weren't going to sell well. That meant we stocked them in some stores and not others, which required complicated ordering and inventory procedures to keep track of exactly what we had, and where.

It could only last so long. When we formed the goal of 1000 stores in 20 years, it became clear we had to streamline the operation as much as possible. If we couldn't have the same stock in all the shops, something had to give.

Antique and estate jewellery were good for the image of the company — they helped move us away from the 'discount' label — but after some soul-searching, we decided to let the antiques go. It was a sad decision, but we had to remember the main goal: if we are ever to get to 1000 stores, we need to keep our formula as simple and straightforward as we can.

Incidentally, it was a good example of how having a broad, overarching goal can make running a business easier: the decision we were procrastinating about suddenly became a very clear choice.

At Michael Hill International (the registered name of the company), we always try to stay true to the values of the original family business we grew from. That means we hold our ethics and responsibilities dear, and we set great store by transparency and honesty. The family nature of our business, however, can make things very complicated. When my daughter Emma started in the business, she had to prove herself to the same standards we expected of any other employee. There was no special protection for her, even though as a father I naturally wanted her to be happy and to succeed.

I've consciously had to restrain myself from helping Emma over hurdles, or shielding her from the tougher parts of the corporate world. That's been hard at times — but she is naturally brilliant, and has proved to her old man she can do anything better and faster and bigger. That was always my hope — but hiring her was a big risk.

I am really proud of how well Emma has fitted into the family business. As a little girl, she would work in the Whangarei shop on Saturday mornings, sell a few pieces — under the watchful eye of our real sales staff, of course — and earn a little money to put into her bank account. But as she grew older, it became clear she wanted a real role in the business.

After finishing school in Brisbane, Emma did a Bachelor of Commerce degree at the University of Queensland, then travelled for a while in Europe. Throughout her education, she continued working in our stores in the afternoons and at weekends, slowly developing sales skills, just as I had learned at the elbow of my father.

By the age of 22 — after the requisite stint sharing a loo with 16 other New Zealanders in a dodgy flat in London — Emma was back in Brisbane and keen to work at Michael Hill.

'Well, you'll have to have an interview, just like everyone else,' I said. 'Go and see Mike Parsell.'

Emma lined up an interview with Mike, our CEO, and went off in her best clothes, eager to impress. I think everyone in the company was a little bit uneasy about this. She was family — my beloved daughter — so how could she possibly not get special treatment?

I knew Emma was determined to succeed, and I knew she was immensely bright and capable — but I was determined not to intervene in her career. I remembered the days of working for my uncle. With every setback and disappointment, I became stronger and more determined, and I knew that would also be the case with Emma. The hands-off policy was hard. Many times I would privately despair: 'Maybe Emma's not getting a fair go. Are they being too tough on her?' Nevertheless, I never interfered. It's difficult for a dad to stand back — especially when he knows that some of the staff are making life difficult for his daughter by making the natural assumption that she has been handed her career

Emma Hill with her proud parents at her new Robina store, 1994.

on a silver platter.

The initial interview went well, and Mike said he was keen to hire Emma. We rotated her around the stores for a while then, after a couple of years, Mike made her manager of a new store in Robina, on Queensland's Gold Coast.

'She doesn't have to be as good as everyone else,' Mike used to say. 'She has to be better. She has to work harder, and make sure everyone around her can see she's up for it.'

Sounds harsh, doesn't it — but Mike's philosophy was that Emma just couldn't afford to fail.

After managing Robina well, Emma moved on to manage a few of our higher-volume stores. But she was desperately keen to take on a bigger role. Mike didn't think she was ready, so Emma, thinking ahead as always, decided to do a Masters of Business Administration at Bond University in Brisbane. After a year of full-time study, she graduated with distinction and gave the valedictory address for the whole university. What a proud moment — my mother Billie and I sat in the audience, hugely impressed and moved by this bright young lady.

Emma at her graduation for her MBA.

At the time, Christine's father was very ill in hospital in Whangarei, and neither he nor Christine could attend the ceremony. So Emma flew over to see him and delivered her valedictory speech to him right there in his hospital room with Christine, her grandmother Dorothy and the nurses watching. It was a very moving experience.

The degree gave Emma a chance to pause. Rather than

coming straight back to Michael Hill after graduating, she took a job at the Sydney advertising agency Lew Deegan, which managed our account.

By this stage, the late 1990s, our advertising had become too predictable and felt stale. We certainly had name recognition, and I was still presenting the ads, but the board felt the brand was perceived as cheap — a concept we were keen to move as far away from as possible.

So Emma and Lew came to us with the suggestion that Emma take over as the face of the brand and front the advertising. She took elocution lessons in preparation, and was very excited about the prospect. I thought it was a great idea, but it didn't eventuate and after a while we decided the ad account should go out to tender to see if we could flush out some fresh thinking.

We asked several ad agencies to pitch ideas, and Emma led the pitch for her agency. The board didn't like it. At any rate, they didn't like it as much as the pitch from a rival agency, McCann Erickson, which had a concept based on playing up the emotion of a jewellery purchase: the sentimental choice of an engagement ring, a wedding band, an anniversary ring, a christening gift.

I'm sure you can imagine how it felt as a dad, when my lovely daughter gave a stunning presentation to the board, and was rejected. It was one of the worst days of my life. I had to call her myself and break the news.

'Emma,' I said, 'I'm sorry, but we are going with the McCann proposal.'

I was a complete wreck. Emma was devastated. She cried with her girlfriends, felt terrible and resigned from Lew Deegan. Michael Hill had been one of their major accounts and although Lew wanted Emma to stay and work on other campaigns, she felt it was time to move on.

Shortly afterwards, a new position opened up at Michael Hill International, that of marketing executive. Emma decided that with her experience she would be perfect for the job and so put in her CV, wrote a covering letter, and was interviewed by Mike Parsell.

She did not get the job. Again, Mike did not feel she was ready.

But, thank God, he thought there was something she was ready for: launching our business in Canada.

That was the great thing about my hands-off policy: I couldn't save her from the disaster of the ad pitch, and I couldn't get her the job she wanted — but I could stand back and watch her get another, far more exciting job without any influence from me at all.

She was chosen fair and square by Mike and her peers. There was no doubt about it this time. So, at the age of 31, Emma was instructed to prepare her own team and launch Michael Hill Jeweller in Canada. It was a dream come true for her.

Going into Canada was the first big step in the direction of 1000 stores. Why Canada? Well, we needed to go somewhere. We can't have 1000 stores in Australasia; there simply isn't a big enough population. While we have often considered expanding into the United Kingdom, there are complicating issues there involving hallmarking. We wanted somewhere in the northern hemisphere where English was spoken and where we could communicate for at least a few hours during the day. The US, at that time, was considered too difficult for a first stop, so Canada it was.

Emma and her team moved to Vancouver in August 2002 and at the end of October opened the first Michael Hill store,

Top: Original start-up team in the snow, Vancouver, 2002.
Bottom: It doesn't take long to fit out a new store. New Canadian stores were up and running in about 20 days.

to be followed by two more before Christmas of that year. It doesn't take that long to open a store, interestingly enough. The longest lead time is in finding leases and negotiating terms. With all our experience, and a close eye kept on cost effectiveness, we can now fit out a shop from start to finish in 20 days.

Emma must have been a bit daunted to be thrown in the deep end like that, but she had a lot to prove. Just like Christine and me, all those years before, Emma found the hard, fast years terribly exciting and challenging. She never doubted it would be a success — and nor did we.

She did realise, however, why Mike Parsell had been so hard on her. The Canada adventure showed Emma how raw and frightening it is to launch a business. She could see why Mike wanted her to be ready — really ready — before she took on a major role in the company. In retrospect, she agrees with his decisions. You might think, given their history, that Emma and Mike would have a testy relationship. In fact, the opposite is true — Emma has enormous admiration for Mike and likes him immensely, and the feeling is mutual.

Like me, Emma has always been goal-oriented and when she was living in London she read a book by the motivator Tony Robbins, after which she wrote down that she would like to open Michael Hill in a new country within 10 years. At the time of writing down her goal, she assumed that country would be the UK but, nearly 10 years later, she was in Vancouver, after fighting tooth and nail to achieve her goal, opening Michael Hill in a new country.

The move also changed her life personally. While scouting the country for store locations, she met Canadian Doug Jacques, a real estate broker. They had a business relationship for a couple of years, and then it developed into quite a bit more. They're now married, with twins.

The Canada experiment worked very well — and I believe that's because Emma is truly passionate about the business. She never got any favours, and never expected any, and so she was more than up for the challenge of tackling the inevitable roadblocks and hostilities a new business must encounter in a foreign land.

We have stores in Alberta and Ontario now, too. We open them in clusters because it's critical to the success and ease of training and development (remember Canberra?), which are crucial when you become a larger operation. It's also crucial, when you have a long-term goal like ours, that you do not expect instant successes. Emma never has — and that's why she has succeeded.

Michael Hill staff story: Emma Hill

Regional manager, Canada

Mum and Dad have taught me many things over the last 37 years. They are great role models and I have tremendous respect and admiration for what they have achieved. Together they have created a great balance of health, wealth and happiness.

One of the toughest and most valuable lessons they have taught me is perseverance. You haven't failed until you quit. Whether running a marathon, opening a new business, or teaching one-year-old twins not to throw their dinner on the floor, if you persevere you will succeed.

I've been very fortunate with my upbringing. I've been raised in a loving family environment with down-to-earth values. I've had the freedom to set and pursue my own goals with the support and encouragement of my parents. And while I have grown up in what would definitely be considered to be a well-off family, I haven't had it too easy. Whether it was buying my first car, a white Datsun Sunbird riddled with rust, or getting the opportunity to expand the jewellery brand overseas, I've had to work hard to make my goals happen. If things come too easy in life you never develop the strength required to cope with adversity and reach your full potential. Besides it's the journey that's the fun, and the destination is all that much sweeter when you've had to push damn hard to get there. So if you are going through a rough patch, remember that you haven't failed until you quit.

Dad's always preached the value of goal-setting and its something I've adopted. You've got to know where you are heading in order to get there. I find that when you have created and committed yourself to an exciting future, every day has more meaning and purpose. One of the biggest goals I had previously set myself was to successfully establish Michael Hill Jeweller in a new market within 10 years. I still have the original piece of paper I wrote this on 16 years ago back in London. My next goal was to get the Canadian business to break even and return home to start a family within five years. I was keen to stop Dad's jokes about me being an old maid left on the shelf, and so I think everyone was quite relieved when the marriage goal was also achieved. I've now got new goals that will guide my next 10 years and beyond so thanks to Dad's lectures on goal-setting, life is always pretty exciting.

I think reading really helps you get ahead and get an edge on your competition. You gain wisdom by reading the right books. So, rather than relax at the end of the day with a romantic novel, I like to relax with a book that's going to help get me ahead. I've picked up the habit of reading meaningful books from my parents. Mum reads biographies. Biographies are amazing books that immerse you in someone's life and allow you to learn from their experiences and see the world through their eyes. Dad reads business books, from which you can glean great insight into how other companies tick and learn from their successes and failures. I read a combination of both.

The first business book I read was *How to Win Friends and Influence People* by Dale Carnegie. Dad calls this book his bible and I agree, it's a must-read. I'm currently reading *The Snowball*, Warren Buffet's latest book on the business of life. The more you read, the more you know. It's quite a simple formula for getting ahead!

I'd like to thank Mum and Dad for everything they have done for me over the last 37 years. Having just had kids of my own, I now have a true appreciation of the immense commitment they have both made to get me to where I am today.

Michael Hill staff story: Mike Parsell
Chief executive officer

After growing up in Kawakawa, a small country town in the north of New Zealand, I left school at 15 years of age. Impatient with school and anxious to get out into the real world I convinced my father to allow me to leave school in exchange for helping him with a large contract painting the local dairy factory. After trying my hand at various things, I entered the jewellery industry as an apprentice watchmaker. Watchmaking taught me the importance of detail and process. However, it also taught me there was more to life than looking into the back of a watch!

An advertisement appeared in the local paper for a store manager for Michael Hill Jeweller, so I applied. The day of the interview I remember arriving in the store only to be kept waiting. There was a commotion going on out the back and it seemed a mistake had been made and I wasn't actually supposed to be there! Finally I was interviewed by Joke Jansen, the senior sales professional, who then convinced Michael to interview me. It turned out that on realising I was a watchmaker he had refused to see me! Michael had also started his career as a watchmaker and had little time for them.

I spent two years working in the Whangarei store, learning

the art of selling and retailing before being offered my first management position at age 24.

Along with my wife Rosanne and our newborn baby we embarked on our first adventure, moving to Takapuna, Auckland. We were given the task of turning the store around or moving it to Palmerston North. After visiting Palmerston North I came back with an absolute determination to never live there! Takapuna's annual sales were less than half a million per year and within three years sales had grown to $3 million. The company then floated in 1987, and I was offered a chance to spearhead the growth to Brisbane as the Australian general manager.

Australia was not easy, particularly in the early years when we were both settling into a new country and trying to succeed in a fiercely competitive market. However the business quickly gained momentum. It was in this role that I learned the importance of building the right team around you and of perseverance! I was appointed to the board in 1989, became joint managing director in 1996 and CEO in 2000.

I have had the privilege to lead an amazing team of passionate and determined people who have all shared a quiet resolve to make Michael Hill Jeweller an international success story. I have seen so many people exceed their own expectations and smash their own glass ceilings. As the company has expanded into Canada and the US it has been so rewarding to see people rise up through the company and embark on their own international adventures.

Recently I had the privilege of presenting our first million-dollar sales professional a brand-new BMW 320i convertible at a ceremony in Auckland. It was one of the proudest moments of my career. For years we had dreamed of the day we would have our first sales professional break the million-dollar threshold. This seemingly impossible feat was achieved by an amazing lady who, through sheer determination and an unwavering resolve, did what was necessary, day by day in order to win her prize. The story she told that night about what she had been through to achieve her goal was inspirational because it demonstrated that anyone can succeed if they have a mind to.

Michael Hill has a culture which allows ordinary people to accomplish the most extraordinary things. In my 28 years with the company, I have seen so many people exceed goals they never once would have thought possible — both in their careers and in their personal lives.

We have learned what can be achieved when good old-fashioned hard work is combined with a little common sense and a huge dose of perseverance. This is especially so when those efforts are charged and aligned within a culture that shares a powerful and audacious vision. Ours is a company that has constantly challenged people to be the best that they can be, where the thrill of the chase and the feeling of accomplishment have you coming back for more — time and time again!

People sometimes overlook retail as a career. That saddens me. It is an amazing industry with so many different disciplines to master. The art of selling, communication and leadership, of being a merchant, a buyer, a marketer, a trainer, a sales manager, a recruiter — all these things combine to create one of the most challenging and rewarding careers I know. It still has me leaping out of bed every day anticipating the challenges that need to be overcome — even after 30 years! I still clearly remember the buzz of selling my first 10-carat diamond in 1987. I didn't sleep for two nights!

Stradivarius

As a boy I dreamt of being a professional violinist. Although that dream never came true, I did manage to have some serious fun with violins.

I've always kept up my playing, I've taught some people, and I've even bought and sold a few instruments in my spare time. I am a salesman, after all, so what could be more natural than combining my two greatest passions: violins and selling. I got a great kick out of it. Sometimes I had to do them up a little, give them a polish to make them shine, add new strings, put them in a new case and then I could flick them off for a handy profit.

I love to play JS Bach, my favourite composer. His solo partitas and sonatas are the Everest of violin music. Every time I play those, I see another way to express myself in a way that no other music does. It is a great way to lose myself in another world.

On a visit to England, I dragged Christine to visit Beare's violin shop in Wardour Street. Charles Beare is probably the greatest violin expert in the world, one of the few people who can work out exactly where a violin comes from. It's not easy — many violins are falsely labelled by dealers who try to pass off second-rate instruments as the handiwork of renowned craftsmen. Even top-quality violins are often mislabelled, because over the centuries details have got lost and confused — for example, I own a Giovanni Dollenz instrument that somehow got mislabelled as a Guadagnini.

The most sought-after label of all is that of Antonio Stradivari, the seventeenth-century Italian violin maker, whose instruments today sell for up to several million dollars each. Stradivari only made 1100 instruments in his lifetime and around 700 have survived — but I'm sure I've met many more than 700 people who think they own one. These violins are usually cheap imitations that were factory-made by the millions.

This is where Charles Beare comes in. He's a genius at identifying instruments, and has helped me sort out the provenance of a few instruments, so I was keen to meet him in person when I next went to London.

'Would you like to play a Stradivarius?' Charles asked that day. Of course I would. It was a life-changing experience: rich and sweet and vibrant. The workmanship was faultless.

You can guess what's coming: I fell in love with that sound, and over the ensuing decade, I gradually decided I wanted a Stradivarius of my own. It became one of my goals.

Yes, I did buy one, eventually. I bought it over the phone, unseen — which is fairly unusual, they tell me. I never laid eyes on the violin until we caught up with the dealer in Salzburg the following year for the handover.

In our hotel room, he opened up the case and handed me this amazing 315-year-old violin. I picked up my bow and gave it a try. It was pure perfection.

After a week of musical delights, Christine and I came back home, but the Stradivarius stayed in Europe.

Christine thought that was crazy — but I felt the violin was worthy of a better player, and in reality everything you own is only on loan. You are the custodian for the future generations.

Now the violin is in the safe hands of Feng, the incredibly talented Chinese violinist who won the Michael Hill International Violin Competition in 2005. He is extraordinarily talented, and it was clear to me he needed an extraordinary violin to really match his ability. I decided to loan him my Stradivarius.

We had the violin delivered to Feng at the end of 2007. People would leap to their feet with tears in their eyes when this young man played the 1694 Stradivarius.

What's extraordinary is that this violin, as far as we know, had never been played by a true virtuoso until Feng got hold of it. So despite the fact that it's more than 300 years old, it needed breaking in. The experts will tell you that the wood of a violin has a memory, so when a great violinist plays a Beethoven sonata, the next person who plays the same sonata reaps the benefits

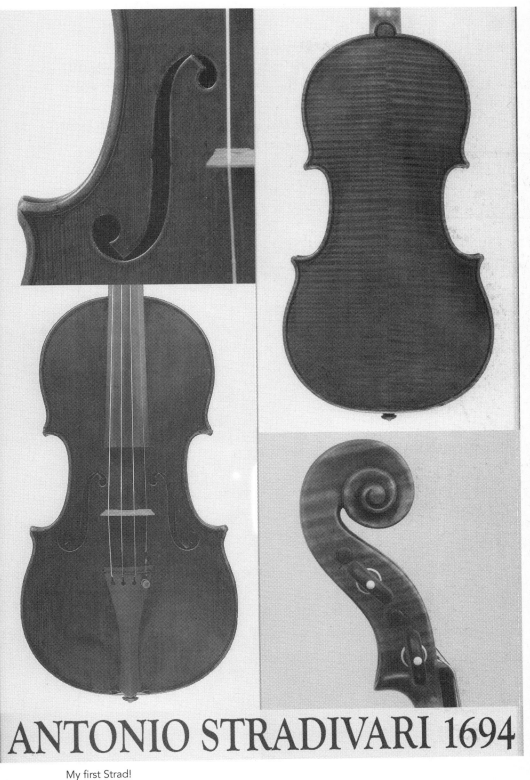

ANTONIO STRADIVARI 1694

My first Strad!

because the memory of the music is implanted in the wood of the violin and comes out in the sound. Feng tells me it's sounding better every day.

So even though it didn't end up being my career, my love for music has brought another dimension to my life.

Always pursue what you love.

Always extend your talents.

Never abandon your dreams.

Genius is one per cent inspiration,
99 per cent perspiration.
Thomas A Edison

Chapter 11

START AT THE BOTTOM

Welcome to the company. Now, back to the shop floor you go.

When anyone joins Michael Hill International as an executive, they learn one lesson very fast: there's no opulent management lifestyle in our company. If you want to stroll plush-carpeted corridors and look important while holding a briefcase, we're not the right fit for you.

My firm belief is that nobody can succeed in any business without understanding — at a real and practical level — the very fundamentals of it. That means the factory floor, the farm gate, the shop floor, and it means getting one's hands decidedly dirty. It's a fairly simple principle, but you'd be amazed how frequently businesspeople forget their responsibility to understand the way an enterprise works from the ground up. Central business districts around the world are full of office towers packed with people who work for companies with which they have no practical connection. There are literally floors upon floors of executives in suits working for telecommunications giants or accountancy firms or mining conglomerates, but they wouldn't have the first clue how to patch a telephone exchange, or fill in a tax return, or dig some gold out of the ground.

That's not good enough.

With a business grounded in retail like Michael Hill Jeweller, it's straightforward enough to see the mental connection between the real business and management: the real business is the shops, which bring in the money by selling jewellery, and the executives support that enterprise.

In some firms there's a greater gap. A big mining firm, for example, houses its executives in a city building that is a thousand kilometres away, literally and figuratively, from the holes in the ground that constitute the real business. I can understand how those mining execs might forget what the business is really about, but I don't think it's a good way to conduct a business. As the mining boom ends, and the

Christine painting head office, 1986.

economic downturn bites, perhaps we'll see a few people learning this lesson: ah, fellas, maybe we should have been a bit closer to the ground all along.

All Michael Hill managers and executives have to start at the coalface, and keep going back. Everyone who wants to rise high in our company needs to know how to sell a diamond ring, and have plenty of practice at it. That's what we're all about, after all.

I've discovered many of the people who apply for jobs with our company are straight out of university, having completed marketing or business degrees. They know a lot about management theory and the latest respected texts on capital flows, but they wouldn't have a clue how to run a decent small business. Our company is comprised of many, many small businesses, after all. We might be linked by an umbrella structure, and have common goals and strategies, but no store will survive unless it is slick and profitable and efficient as a stand-alone business.

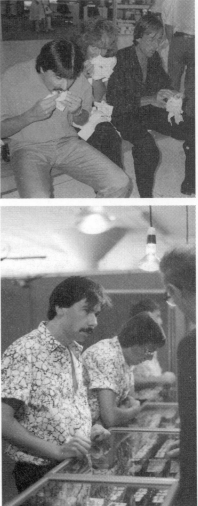

So why is it so important to learn how a shop works? Because that's the essence of understanding people: not just the customers and what they want and don't want, but also the staff. In a compact environment like a shop, all the issues and problems of personality and delegation and inter-relationships are crucial. A manager is tested to the extent of his

Top: Mike, Christine and I grabbing a bite to eat between store visits, February 1987. Bottom: Mike and I selling. Notice how Mike is looking at the customer's eyes.

or her ability. To coin a phrase, there is nowhere to hide: your staff will be well aware of all your foibles and flaws, and won't hesitate to let you know if you're not up to the leadership gig. And it's good to find out all of that stuff before the stakes are too high: if you can't inspire and motivate a team within a shop, you certainly won't be able to run a company.

Our firm is full of people who have risen through the ranks from the very bottom. There's our CEO Mike Parsell, whom we hired in Whangarei in the very earliest days. He wanted to learn how to sell, so I taught him everything I'd learned from my father. It turned out Mike had a gift; not just for sales, but for managing and motivating people. Today, he is as integral to the success of Michael Hill Jeweller as I am.

My own daughter Emma Hill worked her way up from casual shop assistant to head of our expansion into Canada, and had to prove herself countless times along the way. Another former shop manager, a young fellow named Darcy Harkins, now runs our fledging United States division — an extremely exciting challenge. And one of my favourite stories of all is of Galina Hirtzel, who started as a salesperson on our shop floors, proved herself a savvy and tough negotiator, and is now our head buyer. Travelling the world buying diamond jewellery is really a pretty sensational vocation.

My own experience of learning from my father, I believe, has been the foundation of my own success. As Dickie's apprentice, I found my calling. I had never wanted to be a salesman, and was only made Dickie's junior because my uncle hadn't a clue what else to do with me. Working with Dickie was the first great learning experience of my business career: no matter how big or important your business gets, you are nothing if you cannot sell.

Uncle Arthur was not usually out the front of his store. He

was in the back 'doing the books'. That also meant he spent a lot of time overseas on buying trips. He'd come back from Venice with loads of Venetian glass, for example, or go to Dresden to buy the small porcelain figurines that have made that German town famous. Arthur once returned from India with what seemed to be millions of miniature trophy cups. There was no explanation — he just expected that whatever he unpacked from his trunks, Dickie and I would sell. He was right, too. Dickie could sell anything, and before long those miniature trophies had all marched out the door.

Our ability to identify and harness the power of amazing people has made Michael Hill Jeweller the success it is today. And given that we're expanding rapidly around the world, we're constantly on the lookout for great people. I don't expect many of them to come through universities. It's not that I have any bias against tertiary degrees, or a chip on my shoulder about education — it's just that my experience has shown that the best people come from the shop floor.

I've found far too many bright young people are convinced they need to go to university in order to succeed. If anything, Michael Hill Jeweller is proof this isn't true. There are brilliant careers to be made in retail-based businesses. I don't think it's a drawback that we are so closely connected to the coalface of our business — on the contrary, I think that's what makes retail such an exciting sector to work in. It's about human interaction, about understanding what customers want and don't want, and grasping the trends and currents that are sweeping through our society.

If you're interested in people, retail would seem to me a natural industry to go into. So why don't more young school-leavers think of starting an apprenticeship in a shop? I suspect there might be a bit of fear involved, fear of stepping away from the herd, of doing something that the conventional wisdom doesn't favour right at this moment. I suspect that before too long the mania our Western societies have for higher education might resolve itself to a slightly more sensible level — we'll begin to remember that careers don't need to be based on university degrees to be valid, and return to the wisdom of our parents' generation. They understood that the best experience comes from the university of life. In our case, it's the university of retail.

Today many of our younger trainee managers are too impatient. They want instant success and expect to fly within a few months. The reality is that although it appears simple, becoming a Michael Hill Jeweller manager involves mastering a number of critical things: understanding the product sufficiently; fully understanding our comprehensive selling system, so that it becomes second nature to coach the team on the floor; and becoming a role model for the team, a motivator, an advisor and a friend.

Sales is an art form, and I believe it's one that is seriously overlooked by many retailers. It is dangerous to underestimate the amount of time and practice it takes to really understand sales — at least equivalent to taking a university degree, in my view. My own 23-year apprenticeship might have been slightly too long, but it certainly ensured I was well trained by the time I finished.

So what are the qualities we look for in our staff?

Patience is crucial, as are dynamism, diligence, integrity and passion. All of that takes a long time to prove. Even if we feel a young manager has demonstrated all the qualities we believe are integral to success, it takes a long time to understand all the systems we've established: selling, inventory, staff management, and many more.

To go from trainee to manager takes many months, if not years. Some of our best people have worked their way up very, very slowly — but that's all right. It's not a race. It's about moving people up only when they are ready, and encouraging them every step of the way.

Emma, my daughter, understands that only too well. She thought she was ready for the task well before she was chosen, and is grateful now that she spent so long learning the Michael Hill Jeweller way before she managed a store. When she came to run an entire country, it was all second nature to her. It felt more instinctive than learned — and that's exactly the way it should be. When things started stumbling and scraping, as they inevitably do, she was able to call on her instinct and her intrinsic understanding of the business to get her through. And she did, to my enormous pride.

Another attribute of a brilliant manager is that he or she is always on the lookout for more top people. I always looked for the very best I could find, as I knew that the stronger the team, the less effort I'd have to expend on bringing them up to standard. There's nothing to fear from talented staff, contrary to what some misguided managers seem to think. In fact, if you choose the right team, they'll lift you — and the profit — up with them.

But here's the danger: get the team dynamic wrong and you will all hit the wall together. So, a great manager quickly learns that one of the most important skills is to sift out the maybes, the nearlys and the almost-good-enoughs. To get a great crew, it's crucial to be able to eliminate the candidates who aren't passionate or dedicated enough or simply don't have the right personalities for the job.

The 1991 Australian managers' conference — we had 33 shops at that time.

We don't just let our managers flounder when they strike trouble, however — and that is another key part of our philosophy of sending everyone back to the frontline. At every point, our managers are given help and guidance and support to carry themselves and their teams along. That's only fair. If you're going to send managers out into the field, you have to be firmly behind them like a well-organised invading army, sending supplies, ammunition and reinforcements — and the odd care package — when necessary.

There's another characteristic that makes someone an ideal Michael Hill Jeweller staffer: the X-factor. Sorry to be so vague, but there is undeniably a special something that gives our brilliant leaders the ability to shine. It's hard to define in a single phrase, but you know it when you see it. It's probably similar to what makes a great teacher: passion, enthusiasm, charm, humour and a great deal of determination. Combined, those traits inspire everyone else — and that is good for the whole company.

I'm enormously proud of the brilliance of our people, and I'm happy to boast about them. Why wouldn't I be? It's baffling to hear entrepreneurs and CEOs who seem disparaging of or who are somehow threatened by their top staff. If your team shines, so will you — that's my view, and so far it's worked for me.

Whenever I meet one of our stars-in-the-making, it makes me feel humble. I'm thrilled they've chosen to work with us, and I'm excited about what they can bring to the company. Sensing a winner is a great feeling — a spine-tingling instinct that success is just around the corner. It's terribly rewarding.

So if you are the right person for Michael Hill Jeweller, it won't be difficult to see you coming. I have always believed in gut instinct and I think more of us need to trust our hunches when making decisions. There's a great deal to be said for using this to identify star employees. It's much more effective than relying upon the judgement of some anonymous human-resources 'expert' at a recruitment agency.

Weak managers usually employ staff weaker than themselves, so they can avoid being challenged or shown up. A weak manager might have the best sales record of anyone in the store, but they never fully train their crew, for fear someone might humiliate them. They are usually hopeless delegators and end up trying to do everything themselves — truly jacks of all trades, masters of none, and usually out the back instead of out on the floor training and coaching the team.

When I started my first store in Whangarei in 1979 I realised that the only way I was ever going to succeed was by employing only the best people available, people who were all capable of running the business themselves, I believed. That idea is still at the heart of our company today. If we're going to achieve our goals I need people who are just as passionate and committed as I am.

So where do we find these brilliant people? Wherever they happen to be lurking. They might be working in a hotel, in a restaurant, in another shop, or drinking coffee. They are everywhere.

Smiles from some of our Gold Club members, 2007.

If you know what to look for, you'll see it: a spring in the step, a determined look in their eye, a radiance, an aura and presence that cannot be disguised.

I can't help yawning when I hear businesspeople moaning that it's impossible to find good staff. What a load of rubbish. If you can't find a decent employee, your existing staff won't stay with you, and you can't trust them to be left alone — maybe you're the problem.

You might be hiring the wrong people in the first place. You may be crushing them with a lack of ability to delegate. You could well be strangling their creativity by failing to motivate them properly. Or you may be just too blind to see that within your own organisation, there are stars waiting to shine. If you're not looking closely at them, talking to them about their dreams, sharing your vision and seeking

Awards night at the Noosa conference, 2001.

constantly to understand them, you'll never know how talented they might be — and that's a terrible waste.

Once you've found your talented people, it's crucial to encourage them to form their own goals, and to envisage their success, just as they're encouraged to envisage the success of the company as a whole. We have a system called the Michael Hill Gold Club. This is a group of our 100 top salespeople, who are motivated by a system of rewards that can make individuals very wealthy indeed. The group is enormously competitive about sales figures, and each year the announcement of who's in first, second and third place is eagerly awaited throughout the organisation.

These serious salespeople will tell you that throughout the year they actually envisage themselves at our end-of-year party, being fêted in front of everyone else. They visualise their rewards. They paint a very clear picture of what they are working towards and they get it. And that's what makes them different from the average plodders, those who just come to work, do their daily duties and go home again. If they don't have goals or targets in mind, they're never going to achieve highly — and that's what makes our Gold Clubbers different from the rest.

In every shop, we have a chart monitoring the sales figures of each staff member, with targets based on improving sales from the previous year. At the end of each week, every salesperson can mark on their chart whether they fell below their target (red dot), landed right on it (black dot) or shot ahead of it (gold dot). Not only does this make it clear to each person how well they are doing for themselves, it makes it clear to other salespeople in the shop — always good for competition — and allows the manager to see at a glance who is doing well, and who might need help.

In similar ways, we trace the performance of every store, region and country, so we know instantly where we are doing well, and where we are falling behind.

Having goals in black and white in front of you like that can make all the difference to your ability to achieve them. If one week is lacklustre, it's possible to see immediately that a problem is developing, analyse what's going wrong and correct it. The next week, it'll be clear whether the medicine took effect.

Here's another instance where I believe it is crucial to start from the bottom: when you are starting your own business. If you decide your goal is to begin afresh, the only way to guard against failure is to inform yourself. You need to get in at the ground floor of your chosen industry to really get up close and examine it.

That means you'll need to begin working for someone else who is already in the field. If you want to set up your own coffee shop or importing business, it's crucial to go and work for an existing coffee shop or importing business. It doesn't matter where you get your start — you could be sweeping the floor. The important thing is to observe, observe, observe. Notice everything: the systems, the staff situation, the workflows, the inventory — absolutely everything.

When you feel you understand the way the business works, then — and only then — are you ready to start out on your own.

Michael Hill staff story: Leah Hurst

Regional manager, New South Wales North

My exciting international career with Michael Hill started 10 years ago. When I began I knew nothing about fine jewellery — other than I loved a little sparkle!

I spent my first months mastering my selling skills, enjoying the great company culture and focusing hard on my business degree. During my manager training, I met Emma Hill at a development camp. She was about to open Michael Hill stores in Canada and she convinced me to go. After 18 months of begging her to give me a store, she finally did.

The next step for me was regional management and a new province. I opened my first store as a regional manager in Alberta. The weather was –22 degrees Celcius that day, but the store looked fabulous and the customers loved what we had to offer. Before I knew it, five years in Canada had passed and home, Australia, was calling.

Life for me has always been about vision and unwavering focus on your goals. My experience with Michael Hill has been a wild, exciting and challenging ride.

Michael Hill staff story: Maretta Beatch

Store manager, Canada

I started with Michael Hill Jeweller in 2005. I was 20 years old and had just come from McDonald's as a team leader, and was due to start as a manager-in-training at Seven Oaks, Abbotsford, British Columbia. I took over my first store two years later. I went from a girl who ran shifts at a fast-food restaurant to a woman who took charge of a failing store in a small town and won the company's Best Overall Financial Award for 2007/2008.

I have developed in many ways: patience, compassion, decisiveness, tact and the ability to adapt to change. The things that have particularly influenced me are:

> Success comes from being the person you choose to be, not the person everyone thinks you are.

> Don't let anyone ever tell you that you can't. If they do anyway, prove them wrong.

Michael Hill staff story: Kathryn Scott

Store manager, Sylvia Park, Auckland

My career with Michael Hill began in 1987 when I joined the first South Island store in Cashel Street, Christchurch. We were the pioneers of the south, as the company was not yet a household name down there. It was an exciting time and couples would come from all over the South Island to purchase engagement rings from us. Soon other branches opened in Christchurch and I was promoted to assistant manager of the Cashel Street store. It was a huge learning curve: I had a great manager, who delegated well; I was able to help open new stores; and I enjoyed the management training and development opportunities.

Eventually, I was appointed manager of the Newmarket store in Auckland, then the next stage for me was running the large- format stand-alone store in Mt Wellington. This was truly a destination store because it had no passing foot traffic. The dynamics were totally different: the store was both elegant and big, and a large staff was needed to operate it. It was a wonderful environment to work in and a pleasant experience for the customers, with couches, coffee, a play area for the children and privacy for those who wanted it.

After seven years, the decision was made to relocate into the new Sylvia Park shopping centre, the largest in the country at that time. It was quite a transition moving from such a large space into a small corner site. However, the team adjusted quickly and the results have proved that it was a wise and profitable move.

It's a funny thing in life:
if you accept nothing but
the best, you often get it.
Oscar Wilde

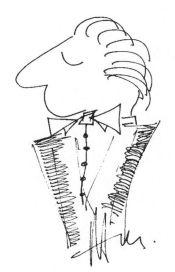

Chapter 12

PRESENT YOURSELF
PERFECTLY

If there's a sure way to undermine yourself as a salesperson — and an entrepreneur — it is this: look sloppy and messy. Have bad breath. Keep your workplace — or your shop counter — messy and disorganised. And don't bother about aesthetics: it's what you say that counts, not how you look.

Rubbish. The truth is that presentation is absolutely crucial. I can't overemphasise the importance of making sure that you, and your workplace, look right. It's the key to getting ahead in sales, and in business generally. Because, like it or not, people do judge books by their covers. It's nearly impossible to overlook manifest flaws in appearance. Just think about it: how frequently do you spend the first minute of a news bulletin thinking, Why is the newsreader wearing that? Or staring at a reporter wondering why his hair is blowing all over the place.

Poor presentation is completely distracting, and distractions are a hindrance you just don't need in business, whether you're trying to sell a piece of jewellery or pitch for a million-dollar contract.

So many businesspeople overlook the importance of presentation. For example, let's focus on sales. It's my area of expertise, and it's a topic upon which we're all pretty knowledgeable; after all, we've all spent time looking at products in shops, and deciding whether or not to buy them. So often, I'll see salespeople who are sloppy or lazy in the way they present themselves and their products. In fact, sometimes I think it goes beyond idleness and into the territory of complete disdain for the customer. My products are so crash-hot, they seem to be thinking, it doesn't matter what I do or don't do. They'll sell themselves.

That's nonsense. In fact, every sale is a series of seductions, which at any point can be completely thrown off by poor attention to detail. And exactly the same principles apply no matter what your business is.

First, be aware of where your customers are. Are they walking past your shop window, or looking through the window? If you spot them before they see you, it gives you a huge advantage. A discerning eye will tell you a lot.

Next, you've got to subtly get their attention. Hold it, engage in a non-business conversation and discover what they are interested in. Convince them you're genuinely interested — and genuinely interesting. Make a presentation and, finally, close the deal.

It really should be obvious why presentation is so important in this process, but how often have you been into a shop that's dirty and disorganised, or dealt with salespeople who don't seem to care whether you buy or not, or been turned off an expensive garment because it's crumpled up on a shelf, rather than displayed beautifully on a wooden hanger?

It happens to me all the time. Whenever Christine and I go overseas, we delight in checking out the shops. I love looking at clothes and shoes and, of course, jewellery. I'm not a huge consumer, but I enjoy seeing what's new and interesting in the shops, and I'm always fascinated by how retailers are doing their business.

I'm a pretty unforgiving customer. If anything puts me off about a shop, a product or a salesperson, I'll walk away. Some customers will put up with a lot, and grit their teeth through an amateurish or prickly sales pitch in order to buy an item they really want. I won't — and I suspect the same is true of a great many customers.

On several occasions in the UK I've left a shop without buying, despite being interested in the products, because the staff have put me off. Sometimes it's been the way they sit frostily behind the counter, glaring at customers who come through the door. At other times, I've turned away from a shop window because it's so cluttered and the products so poorly displayed. And there have been occasions when I've tried on a garment or picked up a product for a closer inspection, only to decide the salesperson isn't really all that fussed whether I buy or not. In every instance, I'll just walk out. Why should I reward hopeless salespeople? I work hard for my money and I've no inclination to give it away to people who couldn't care one way or the other about my purchase.

If you think about it, that exact philosophy applies to business. At every step in every business deal, you're trying to charm and persuade and convince. Even if you're the one doing the hiring or approving a contract, you're still under pressure to ensure that you're consistently professional and smooth. If you let this professionalism slip, you've done yourself a great disservice, and eventually you'll find people stop taking you seriously.

Christine and I are both interested in aesthetics, and with her flair for art and my interest in sales, we're naturally inclined to care about the way things are presented. From shop windows to advertising and elaborate presentation folders, we've always put a great deal of effort into the look and feel of our business, and it has paid off.

When I was working at Fishers, I discovered another part of shop work I really enjoyed — the window displays. So I taught myself the art of window-dressing, and found myself entirely absorbed in the task. It indulged my artistic passion. In the original Fishers shop, there wasn't much room for extravagant displays, but eventually Uncle Arthur bought a bigger building further up Cameron Street, with a much greater window frontage. Arthur was quite innovative for his time in some ways and gave the new shop big box-like windows, unusual for Whangarei and practically unheard of for a jewellery shop.

Nobody else was terribly interested in window displays, so the task fell happily to me. I'm sure there was a great deal of eye-rolling and mumbling among the staff about how that odd young Hill boy was spending all his time messing about in the windows, but my displays were attracting attention.

I had started putting less and less stock in the windows. At the time, the fashion was to cram the windows with as much merchandise as possible. I thought it would be interesting to try putting just one or two items on display. At first, it looked shockingly bare — so I began experimenting with props, which I used as backgrounds to accentuate the jewellery.

Once, I put a Union Jack flag in the display, which horrified the local Returned Services Association. They were prompt in marching into the shop to complain. Another time, I used field tiles to display diamond rings. That display made it into the pages of the *New Zealand Woman's Weekly*, quite a big deal for an independent Whangarei shop.

Arthur and the others endured my flights of fancy because they could see the results. They knew an eye-catching display got people stopping in the street — and once they had paused in their passage, the next thing you knew, the till was ringing.

After a while, Uncle Arthur beckoned me aside. 'Son,' he said gruffly, 'from now on, I want you to handle all our advertising.' I was astonished; this seemed not unlike praise, which I never expected from Arthur. From then on, I set myself the task of building relationships with the advertising representatives from the local paper, the *Northern Advocate*, negotiating rates for half- and full-page ads in the daily paper.

Suddenly, I was no longer just a salesman. I was learning how to engage the attention and interest of the public, and to work with the media. Those lessons would shape the rest of my life.

I loved this new responsibility. When my dad and uncle retired, I was able to become far more creative and would run weekly newspaper and radio adverts. At the same time I was experimenting with new styles of newspaper advertising, including spending much larger amounts to buy full-page ads, shouting our message as loudly as possible.

So when we were finally in our own shop, all these lessons could be put into full effect. To attract passers-by, Christine began changing our windows weekly, which was quite a time-

It's all in the presentation — some of my window displays at Fishers in the late sixties and early seventies. The top one won best window display in the world at the 1969 Bulova International Window-dressing Competition.

consuming task. But we weren't just putting rings in boxes, we were experimenting with something we'd only ever done ourselves — using clever props. Hose pipes, watering cans, violins, bottles, barbed wire and jars all came into play; we would even search the beaches for driftwood and rusty iron. With just one or two items of jewellery in each window, innovatively displayed on a prop of some description, and using lighting to create dramatic contrasts, we attracted the attention of passing shoppers who might have had no intention whatsoever of purchasing jewellery. We knew if we could get their interest in the first place, we'd be able to entice them with the beauty of our products — or at least make sure they knew who we were.

Another trick we'd perfected in the Fishers days was showing our work in beautiful folders, a method of presentation that helped our promotions enormously. It was all Christine's handiwork, and it began in 1969 when we heard that the Swiss watch company Bulova was running an international competition for window-dressing.

I did two displays: one featuring a Bulova watch, a violin, a sheet of music and a tuning fork with the caption 'Bulova: tuned to perfection'. The other included a shotgun, decoy ducks and a collection of watches in the slots of a cartridge belt. 'Bulova aims at accuracy' declared the slogan. Christine mounted photographs of the displays in a splendid folder, on which she spent many hours of effort, and we sent it off to Switzerland. The judges declared our entry the best in the entire world, inviting us to claim our prize of a trip for two to Switzerland.

This Bulova win proved quite a big breakthrough with my uncle, as it happened, because if he'd had any doubts about my time spent on displays before then, he certainly never

had any afterwards. He never again grumbled about the amount of time I was spending messing about in the windows.

The folders were our secret weapon; we once even won a caravan in a New Zealand competition, by presenting our entry in a beautiful hand-made folder. Another entry in a gorgeous folder won me a trip to Montreux in Switzerland, as part of an Omega competition to mark its 125th anniversary. When Mark and Emma started school, we taught them how to showcase their work in artistic folders to get attention. A sensational display got Mark into Auckland Grammar, and when we were looking for a school for Emma in Brisbane, she and Christine set to work creating a stunning portfolio of her schoolwork and art, using an eye-catching cover and silver ribbon. Inside the folder were certificates, photographs and other luscious details. The whole idea was that it would stand out on the headmistress' desk from all the other plain A4 manila folders submitted by girls clamouring to get into the school — and it worked.

Top: Accepting the Bulova International Award for Window-dressing. Mr Roseman, a Whangarei travel agent presents me with the tickets for the trip.
Bottom: A caravan won in another competition.

Whether you're trying to get your daughter into a top school, angling for a world trip or just entering your chocolate

An example of our beautiful new store designs, which are being implemented from 2009.

cake into the Easter Show competition, great presentation counts for a lot.

And in the same way, we still hold presentation dear in the business philosophy of Michael Hill International. Part of the secret of our success is that all our shops, no matter where they are in the world, are always consistently and immaculately presented. Whenever we open a store, we renovate it to match our signature look, and overhaul the window displays, sales techniques and internal layouts to ensure they comply with the systems we've developed so carefully over the years.

In the same way, we're now devoting a huge amount of time and energy to working on new store design and jewellery presentation for the future, and methods for how we will present our brand as we reposition ourselves. We want to refresh the company's look, and at the same time create a new perception in the minds of consumers about Michael Hill Jeweller. The two concepts are inextricably linked.

Speak up, man

Believe in yourself. It sounds like a fairly generic, feel-good, wishy-washy piece of advice. But let me tell you how it changed my life — by allowing me to overcome one of my greatest fears.

When I was at secondary school I surprised everyone, including myself, by making quite a good speech in front of the class one day.

'How wonderful,' said my parents, Billie and Dickie, thrilled I seemed at last to be succeeding at something. 'How about entering a speech competition?'

Speech competitions, as any parent of teenagers can tell you, are usually terribly serious and stilted occasions. They involve research, notes and — sadly — the attempt by tortured teens to memorise their monologues and deliver them, in a flood of nerves and embarrassment and angst, as quickly as possible.

My attempt was particularly abysmal. After it, I retreated right back into my shell and never gave another speech. Many years later, when I was managing Fishers jewellery store in Whangarei, someone asked if I would say a few words of thanks at an old boys' function. They were not asking me to be the guest speaker, you understand, just the guy that suggests a round of applause afterwards.

Well, I was so shockingly nervous and worked myself into such a frenzy that I thought I was going to throw up. I was completely terrified. I just couldn't do it. So I didn't do it. I made some excuse and scurried home before the guest speaker said a word.

After that, I would address the staff at Fishers, who numbered about six, but otherwise I avoided public speaking.

Losing my house in a fire, as you will know by now, changed everything. It forced me to give up all my old fears and worries, including my terror of public speaking.

When Michael Hill Jeweller was a young company, we engaged the PR firm Hill and Knowlton to do some work for us. They suggested I do some speaking to help publicise our brand. I couldn't say no. I was a new man, fearless and bold — and I had decided to accept the challenges life threw before me, whatever they were.

That didn't mean I was happy about it.

The night before the first speech, which was to a pharmacy guild conference, I started to get fractious. I didn't sleep at all. Some time in the pre-dawn hours, I decided to visualise success. I pictured myself standing up in front of all 400 pharmacists. I saw their faces smiling at me as I pulled it off — and the next day when I was doing it for real, it all came true.

The pharmacists loved me — well, at least they didn't boo me off the stage. I finished my speech without vomiting or fainting, and I think I even sounded reasonably relaxed and engaging. In my mind, it was a triumph.

I couldn't wait to do the next speech — and I eventually became so good at it that people paid me to give motivational lectures at conferences and meetings. Extraordinary, isn't it?

I'll tell you another story about visualisation. I gave a speech in Rotorua recently, and after dinner the organisers announced I was going to demonstrate my golf swing to the crowd. I had had no warning of this, and they had spread a green mat on the ground, and handed me a pitching wedge and a ping-pong ball.

'What's more,' boomed a voice from the speakers, 'Michael will hit the ball through the basketball hoop!'

I stared up at the hoop, which I'd failed to notice until then. Everyone stared at me as they finished off their dinner; I find the general public assumes I'm a brilliant golfer.

There was no choice: I envisaged that ping-pong ball flying

through the air and going into the hoop. It worked — and the crowd, as they say, went wild.

There is nothing mystical or magical about all this. It's just that I had the confidence to pull it off. By visualising myself as a talented public-speaking, golf-swinging success, I calmed my nerves and avoided panicking — and that meant that I didn't stumble over my words or throw the club across the room or otherwise humiliate myself.

Whether it's business or pleasure, I just don't let negative thoughts into my mind.

'What would you do if it all fell apart tomorrow?' I was asked the other day.

I thought it was a funny question. It won't fall apart. And why would I waste my time thinking negative thoughts about what would happen if it did? I would much rather spend my time imagining how to make sure it succeeds.

Some people go through life constantly calculating an Emergency Plan B in case Plan A fails.

I prefer to stick with Plan A.

Health, wealth and happiness
only come to those who focus
on all three.
Michael Hill

Chapter 13

KEEP YOUR BALANCE

Do you know the signature Nokia tune, the melodic little mobile phone ring with which all the Finnish company's phones are programmed? Of course you do — everyone knows it. Researchers have found many people instantly feel stressed and nauseous when they hear the tune, even if it's coming from somebody else's phone, even if they're lying on a beach reading a book, far from the office.

It's a fascinating insight into the way our minds work; people have come to associate that apparently innocuous little song with the incessant ringing of their own phones — and therefore with work, and pressure. It's a marketing and PR disaster for the company concerned, but more interestingly, I think it's a disturbing reflection on the way our modern lives are lived.

We are stressed by our own telephones. They make us unhappy, at least at some subconscious, primal level. And I think the reason for that is clear: too many people simply have no idea how to control the stresses of life.

A mobile phone is the ultimate symbol of modern work: portable, inescapable, time-devouring. Do you keep yours lying by your bed at night while you sleep? Does it vibrate in your pocket all through the weekend? Do you find yourself answering calls while trying to cook dinner, or when you are out having a walk with your children, or in the middle of a deep conversation with a friend? If so, my friend, it's time to achieve some balance in your life.

This book is all about business and the world of work. But I firmly believe that without time for the rest of life, you will never be a real success in your professional life. Working too many hours, eating junky food late at night at your workstation, going weeks without exercise because you simply haven't the time — these are all symptoms of something going seriously wrong in your life.

I know this is the opposite to the conventional wisdom about work, and probably not what you'd expect someone like me to say. I've built a business out of hard slog, after all. But I would have none of this if I didn't also have the ability to switch off from work, divorce myself from the demands of the office and just chill out. Henry Ford's most famous quote was: 'You can have it in any colour you like, as long as it's black.' But the American automotive pioneer also had something very insightful to say about modern life — and even though he said it in the early years of the twentieth century, it's still relevant today.

'The more you think,' said Henry, 'the more time you have.'

He's right. Inspiration is not going to strike at 11.43pm as you frantically send emails while eating a hamburger with one hand. You're never going to forge something brilliant if you are trying to answer emails on your BlackBerry every minute of the day. And if your body is unhealthy, there is no way your mind can be clear or fresh.

I believe balance is the essence of success. Finding an equilibrium of work, health, recreation and relaxation isn't easy — but it will bring you untold benefits. Talk to the top business leaders of the world, and the great majority will tell you how they make time every day for exercise, carefully watch what they eat and strictly limit the time they spend on mobile phone or email communication.

I'm the same. Every day I strive to avoid wasting time on unnecessary things, remember my physical and emotional health, and enjoy the simplicity of life — fresh air, uncluttered time and the freedom to sit around and just think. I'm not pretending this has always been my philosophy, or that I'm perfect at it. I've had to learn the hard way that balance is important. There have certainly been times in my life when I've worked too many hours, paid insufficient attention to my wife and children and allowed the stresses of work to sap away my energy or my enthusiasm. But at a certain point, I read about the Pareto principle, also known as the 80:20 rule. This is a simple idea that has become central to many theories about successful business.

Most things are unequal — that is the basic principle.

In 1906 the Italian economist Vilfredo Pareto observed that at that time 80 per cent of Italy's wealth was owned by 20 per cent of the people. In other words, the richest people in society controlled most of the economy. Pareto discovered the same thing was true in most countries around the world, and became something of a social justice campaigner.

Later, his concept was taken further by a business commentator called Joseph M Juran. He argued that most situations in business could be reduced to the 80:20 rule: for example, you achieve 80 per cent of your results in 20 per cent of your time.

It's an extraordinarily powerful little idea. Every day, you should assess the tasks in front of you and isolate the 20 per cent that are most important and really need your attention now. The rest you should delegate or deal with later. It sounds deceptively simple, I know — and I can hear you saying: 'But I really need to do all the stuff that's on my to-do list NOW. I can't delegate any of it.'

But that's just your perception — what I'm trying to do is get you to think differently about what's in front of you. Actually, it's impossible to do everything now. You must work out what your priorities are — and you must make a considered assessment. Instead, you'll do what most people do: just churn through the work according to whatever happens to be on top of the pile. And what happens? You don't get a chance to finish anything properly. Another task drops onto the top of the pile, and you scramble around to try to manage that as well. Before you know it, you've got 75 tasks on the go at once — and then your mobile phone rings and sends your brain into meltdown.

By going through the mental exercise of identifying the most important 20 per cent of your workload, you are forcing yourself to focus on what really matters, to make the decisions that most people just never make. It's often very difficult to say 'no' when the boss asks us to do something, or a job falls in our lap, but it is always possible to examine the request carefully and discern the most important parts of it. What's the most important 20 per cent of this task? What can be delegated? What can be done later?

Instead of trying to do 100 things in a haphazard way, you'll do 20 things perfectly — and the benefits of those 20 achievements will flow into the rest of the working day.

I use mobile phones and a computer with caution. My freedom of time is too precious to waste — and I believe simplicity is vital. I hate seeing people striding around cities with mobile phones clipped to their belts, or dangling around their necks on one of those silly lanyards. It looks awful, for a start — and it's showing everyone that you're a slave to work. Instead, take control of your phone: remember, it's a symbol of work, and work should be something you do in a considered, deliberate way. Keep your calls short, be specific, and get off the line — and please, never leave a phone on in free time, thinking time, meditating time or in meetings.

The computer is another potential stalker you can do without — especially now laptops and PDAs are so devilishly tiny and transportable. Have a look at the time you're spending on the computer, and see how much of it you actually need to be doing. Here's another example of where the 80:20 rule can be employed: identify exactly what you need to be doing most on your computer, and do that — then free up the rest of your time to do other things.

I'm not suggesting the 80:20 rule should become your new mantra, or that you should time yourself with a stopwatch. That just creates another stress, and my point is all about reducing the amount of stress in your life. I'm suggesting a way to become more mindful about what you are doing with your time. By sitting down and actually considering what you do, how much time you spend doing it and what results you are getting, you will inevitably end up with a more orderly, tidy, efficient day.

Just be mindful. If we are to give life our best shot, it requires undivided attention — otherwise, your vision will be clouded. Distractions will consume your life. And that's not helping anyone.

A conscious effort to focus time and resources works brilliantly at a company-wide level, too. In 2000 we closed our head office in New Zealand and consolidated the whole shebang in Australia. Instantly, we'd cut out a great deal of duplication and organisational clutter. Previously, we'd had head offices in Whangarei and in Brisbane, each operating quite separately, with very little communication. They didn't even

Me in the Whangarei manufacturing plant we closed after moving head office to Brisbane.

share a computer system and, even worse, they were separately sending staff to the same trade shows, and simultaneously doing separate deals with the same suppliers. Shutting the Whangarei office was the direct result of a considered decision about how we were spending our time and resources, and deciding what we could eliminate.

But we ended up with another problem. In our new giant premises in Brisbane, we grew and grew, filling our purpose-built building with people. Once they all moved in, they screamed for yet more people, and before long we were an unwieldy, bloated organisation.

This is a scary thing that happens in a lot of businesses. The bigger an organisation becomes, the bigger the infrastructure, the more people — the less focus. End result? Too many distractions, the building budget blown sky high, and the bottom line starts to suffer.

So we applied the 80:20 rule again. We thinned out our staff to a more manageable level, and put the building on the market. Very quickly, our overheads were back under control, our eyes back on the jewels.

Here's another example. For a while we had a separate warehouse in Canada to service our stores. It was convenient, but it ended up crammed with far too much stock, clogging our supply chain like a blockage in an artery. So we shut it down and brought it all back to Brisbane.

Again, it was about working out what we really needed, and what we didn't — and that disciplined decision-making created the efficiency that enabled us to go ahead with clarity and focus.

Whenever I see the lights on late at night in one of our offices or stores, I'm not happy. I've never been keen on anyone in our company working exceptionally long hours. I'd much rather people

I'm always encouraging everyone to keep fit. The Whangarei team with some family members at a social run, 1982.

worked a decent 40-hour week and spent the rest of their time at the gym, walking along the beach or relaxing with their families.

Many of our employees take a break during the day and head out for a run together, or zip out for a workout. They always return to the office refreshed and sparkly-eyed. I often do this myself, so I know that when my staff plop back down in their chairs and look at the tasks on their to-do lists, they've got a clear perspective and can identify the most important stuff straight away.

Find your balance in life — take the time to go fishing! Here we are with baby Mark, summer, 1971.

Mindfulness about time gives us time to spare, time to think of the big issues and time to discover the easier way forward. Think about your achievements over the past year, and consider how much time you spent really effectively achieving them — I bet the same will be true for you. Now, if only you could eliminate the time you wasted . . .

You can.

'I don't have enough time!' This statement doesn't reflect the reality of most people's situations. In truth, you can get all the time you need by simply being clever about the way you work. I regularly pause to think about what needs to be done by me, and what I can delegate. So when I see the lights on late at night, I'm anxious that some poor soul is slaving away because they believe that nobody else can do it.

That is never true. In fact, delegation is the key to finding balance — and that's why it's so important to build a great team around you. Delegation is like coaching. You spot the right person in your team, then act like a sporting coach, encouraging and guiding them to do the tasks that need to be done. By constantly watching their progress, correcting the finer points and rewarding improvement, you will not only help their career along — you'll also free up a great deal of your own time, both now and in the future. And if you help your team set their own goals, and then give them the trust and freedom to fly, you'll soon find they are able to achieve more and more — and that will help the entire organisation shine.

By learning to delegate in the early years of our Australian expansion, I got the business ticking over nicely without me. I'd learned that as long as I kept in touch on a regular basis, things would continue to gain momentum and I would

Queenstown — a view of my golf course, next to our family home.

be able to spend my time thinking about the big picture, and planning where we were going and how to get there.

I could only do that because I implicitly trusted all the people I'd trained. I knew they didn't need me looking over their shoulders. They all had their own goals and visions, as well as our corporate vision of advancing the company and becoming bigger and stronger every year.

So Christine and I moved back to New Zealand and settled in Queenstown — the prettiest town imaginable, on beautiful Lake Wakatipu in the South Island. As I've said it's also where we discovered meditation, which has been a real epiphany.

With the clarity and calm I've achieved through mindful meditation, I've found my fears and negative thoughts about life have vanished, to a large extent. I've learned to relax and deal with tension, which has helped enormously to develop my self-esteem and a feeling of wellbeing. It has also given me the ability to free up my time, just by being more mindful about it. I'm freer to tackle the big issues, like coming up with our company's vision.

There's a very simple introduction to all these concepts in a book called *The Three Minute Meditator* by David Harp. It contains 30 simple methods for relaxing and unwinding, and it's a perfect guide for people who suspect meditation is just for hippies who enjoy sitting cross-legged on the floor. In fact, meditation can be part of everyone's life, and you can do it in any position you like!

Have you ever dreamed of floating? It's a recurring dream for me, and has been since I was a small boy. I'm asleep, but see myself rising up from a standing position with my arms by my side and feet together. Effortlessly, I glide over the land, looking down at the houses, roads and people.

Why am I telling you this? Because I've adopted that concept of floating as a way of envisaging my goals. Whenever I've got some alone-time — in bed, walking or running I daydream about floating. I visualise the projects I'm working on and float through them in my mind's eye. If it's a new store or building, I imagine myself gliding through, noticing all the details: doors, windows, lights, counters. This forms an indelible print on my memory — and then it becomes a natural part of my thinking.

Don't believe me? Well, give it a try. Walk yourself into the next 20 years of your life and plan your future. See it in great detail, just as you would love it to happen. Sharpen your senses so that your mind can feel, touch and smell the experience. The most difficult thing to do is see ahead, to actually look into the future and decide what you want to happen. Once you can do that, all your decisions — even the most mundane ones — will become easier and clearer.

It took a house fire to give me a vision of the future I wanted — but once I had that vision, I was finally able to move forward and make it happen.

In an earlier chapter, I mentioned the importance of writing down your goals — and this is the time to do it, once you've cleared your mind and allowed yourself to envisage the future.

Without a purpose in life, it's hard to be optimistic or motivated. It's easy to think: What's the point of all this? Why am I even bothering? That's why I hate the word 'retirement' and everything it stands for.

So often, I hear people saying they can't wait to reach retirement and give up work. Twice in my life, I have been in a situation where I've reached my 20-year goal earlier than I expected, and I've thought: Well, now I can finally relax, stop climbing mountains and just chill out.

It's never worked. Within months — even weeks — I became bored of playing golf or whatever retired people are supposed to do. So now I've given up any wish to retire and lead a life of serenity. It's just not me — and it's so much more fun to dream up more mountains to climb.

Body and soul

I have always been fanatical about fitness and keeping in shape, but over the years I've met many people with exceptional talents who don't recognise the need to exercise and eat well. In my view, those people rarely make it to the top.

Why is that? Because there's a certain level of mental discipline that comes from having a healthy body. If you're self-controlled enough to eat healthily and work up a sweat in the gym, or out on a run, you already know how to discipline yourself for work. But if you always manage to find an excuse for avoiding exercise, or if you regulary stuff your mouth with stodge and fat — 'I don't have time to cook' — you will feel stodgy and sluggish. You'll also be caught in the habits of avoidance and making excuses: It's too hard. I'm too tired. I'm too busy. It's too late. It's too early. I'll do it tomorrow.

Yeah, right.

When I'm alert and full of energy, the ideas flow twice as quickly, so I've always been interested in diet and fitness. Ever since I was a young man, I've been a keen runner, and I've read dozens of books on exercise and health. I've been into all the crazes — aerobics, gyms, you name it.

I tried to take up smoking at one point in my youth. I thought it would be cool to smoke a pipe but I could never keep the bloody thing alight, and cigarettes made me feel sick. Anyway, I'm convinced every cigarette shortens one's life by half an hour — I can't afford the time, apart from anything else.

Around 1978, when Christine and I visited Melbourne for a jewellery conference, we ate at a famous steak restaurant. The next day, when I was still savouring the taste of the meal, I started reading a book by Ross Horne, an Australian advocate of vegetarianism and healthy eating — low salt, no animal fats, no processed food.

We've always been great enthusiasts for new ideas, and

vegetarianism was something we'd been idly considering — so Christine and I became vegetarians for several years. It was difficult to start with, as the food tasted bland and there seemed to be thousands of rules about what we couldn't eat, but Christine perfected the recipes and we stuck with it. Hell — the weight fell off me and I started to look like a stick insect again, just as I had as a boy. I'd never been fat, but I'd put on a few kilos over the years. They melted away.

The next big influence was discovering the work of nutritionist and biochemist Dr Michael Colgan, who espoused regular resistance training and a balanced diet for optimal health. Christine and I realised being even slightly overweight was risky, and set about taking nutrition and exercise very seriously indeed.

I'm sure almost all the weight problems in our society are due to environmental problems — in particular, the ubiquity of over-processed foods. The western diet is deadly. For evidence, we need only see how fast obesity and diabetes rise in newly industrialised societies, where the population suddenly has access to fat- and sugar-laden fast foods and processed goods.

It's not gluttony. The problem is foisted on us by food manufacturers, who have replaced the bulk of our food supply with an ever-growing pile of chemicals. If junk food were banned tomorrow, I'm sure most of the excess fat would simply disappear. Health and longevity would blossom. Many of us don't ever make a conscious choice to eat this rubbish; we're conned into it by outlandish advertising.

Then — gotcha! — we're addicted. Food manufacturers employ the best chemists to extract the sweet, sour, salty and savoury tastes and aromas that most tickle our taste buds, then concoct them into foods that artificially stimulate the appetite because they're so loaded with starches and sweeteners.

Most of the beautifully packaged foods in our supermarkets are just junk. Everything from breakfast cereal to fruit juice has added salt and sugar. Fizzy drinks are just time-bombs of sugar, waiting to catapult our insulin levels into the stratosphere. Almost everything else is clogged with trans-fats or hormones. Where are the simple grains, oils, spices, chemical-free vegetables and organic meats? In the expensive delis or health-food shops and, sadly, far from the suburban reality of most people's lives.

So, for what it's worth, here is my formula for a healthy life:

1. Start the day with a green shake referred to in the book *Green for Life* by Victoria Boutenko. Wow, what an energy boost! It's easy to prepare with a high-speed blender. Blend up the tops of vegetables (they carry all the vitamins) — carrot tops, spinach, silverbeet tops, parsley, mint, celery — with your favourite fruit including a banana and some honey. It tastes cool and will sustain you until at least lunchtime. It might take a few days to get used to the idea, but persevere — it's worth it.

2. Quit smoking, no matter what it takes. Smoking is part of a mind-set and once you can visualise the next 30 years without it, I promise you, you will want to stop.

3. Start a regular fitness programme that includes aerobic, extension and connection, and weight-bearing exercises. A personal trainer is a great idea. Even if you only have one session, your trainer can help you work out a tailored programme that you can do in your own time. After exercise, as an energy boost, have a protein shake of 30mg of ion exchange whey protein isolate, blended with a banana, flax seed oil, 250ml of water and some honey.

4. Get blood tests done to find out about and tweak any mineral or hormonal deficiencies.

5. Take vitamins, morning and night.

6. Give up hard liquor and read *The Wine Diet* by Dr Roger Corder. He advises drinking red wine in moderation.

7. Eat little red meat and more fish and vegetables.

8. Avoid all trans-fats. These are chemically heated oils that have undergone a structural change so that they won't go rancid, and are used widely by the food industry in products like potato chips, biscuits and many other foods. They'll clog up your arteries in no time.

9. Eat lots of fruit every day.

10. Avoid desserts — have a salad instead!

11. Avoid lollies, soft drinks and beverages with added sugar.

12. Get a water filter fitted at home so as not to drink chlorinated tap water.

With a bit of effort, you'll feel a million times better. It takes discipline, but so does anything worthwhile. Good health is priceless, and I don't care how busy you are, you're never too busy to be healthy. So toughen up.

We make a living by what we get,
we make a life by what we give.
Sir Winston Churchill

Chapter 14

GIVE BACK
AND YOU SHALL
RECEIVE

I have an 18-hole golf course in my backyard. I also have an international violin competition in my name. And even though neither golf nor violin have anything to do with jewellery, they are both wonderful for my business — and for me.

This is a story of following one's passions. If you're determined and canny enough to pursue the things you really love, you'll find all sorts of benefits flow to the rest of your life, including your professional affairs.

Hosting the New Zealand Open golf tournament came from my desire to share a beautiful piece of land with the world. The violin competition was designed to encourage everyone to see the beauty of classical music. And now, both are opportunities to help build my company into a high-end brand. These projects are among the world's leading competitions in classical music and sport — and you can't buy publicity like that.

I've always loved the violin, ever since I learned to play as a lonely young boy at school. It was my entrée into the world of music and culture. Although I never fulfilled my childhood dream of becoming a professional violinist, I've always continued playing.

In 1999 I got a wonderful opportunity to play in a cave with marvellous natural acoustics at Gibbston Valley Winery, just outside Queenstown, with virtuoso Miranda Adams from the Auckland Philharmonia. It was an amazing thrill to be playing in front of an audience — my yearning had never quite left me — and the cave was packed. We played a Vivaldi concerto, and I felt on top of the world.

After the concert, Miranda joined Christine and me for a walk on the shores of Lake Wakatipu, and we got talking about how, as a young man, I'd auditioned for the National Youth Orchestra and entered in violin competitions — most of which no longer existed. What a shame, we agreed, that aspiring musicians no longer got to test their mettle in a competitive way. That got me thinking — always dangerous.

'It'd be nice to have a fully fledged violin competition,' I mused. 'Maybe I'll start one myself.'

In conjunction with the Auckland Philharmonia, we investigated what it would take to make a music competition internationally accepted, and in 2001 the first-ever Michael Hill International Violin Competition was held in Queenstown.

Young players from all around the world submitted tapes or compact discs, from which a panel of judges from the Philharmonia chose 18 semi-finalists, who were flown to Queenstown at my expense for preliminary heats, adjudicated by seven top international violinists. The judges were a drawcard in themselves — once news got out about the calibre of our adjudicators, all the world's top young violinists wanted to take part in our competition. All 18 violinists had three days playing in front of the adjudicators and audiences in Queenstown, then went up to Auckland, where the three finalists played with the full orchestra.

It is a musical multi-sport. All competitors play a New Zealand-composed piece, plus a bit of Bach, Beethoven and Paganini. Bach is very musically and technically exact but also full of emotion and Beethoven, who was himself a pianist, wrote very difficult music for the violin! Paganini, on the other hand, was a technical guy with very long fingers who could do anything; he was like a gymnast on the violin.

The first winner was Joseph Lin, a Taiwanese-American soloist who plays a rare Italian violin, which he bought for himself. He proved a wonderful ambassador for the biennial competition, which has blossomed beautifully and is now rated as one of the world's most important competitions.

The violin competition is now in it's ninth year, and gaining reputation on a world scale. It has produced some outstanding winners, two of whom have gone on to win the prestigious Paganini Competition in Genoa.

It's quite a costly affair to

The finalists of the first Michael Hill International Violin Competition, including winner Joseph Lin (far left) with us and Wayne Peters (back), one of our generous competition sponsors.

michael hill
2009 INTERNATIONAL
VIOLIN COMPETITION

18 semi-finalists flown to New Zealand
Entries close 26 November
www.**violincompetition**.co.nz

The Michael Hill International Violin Competition is advertised worldwide through all major music conservatories. Each year a different poster is designed by Mark and Monika Hill.

run, but I get an enormous thrill from seeing these young people given an opportunity that might catapult them into a new world — a world I dreamt of as a youngster, but never got to enter.

2005 Violin Competition winner, Feng Ning. Feng is one of the world's most brilliant violinists.

During the 2005 competition, we also held master classes with our seven adjudicators — some of the world's leading violinists — at the University of Auckland. Here was an opportunity for anyone studying music at the university to get some hands-on experience with a world-class musician.

Speaking of opportunities, let me tell you about the golf course in my backyard. To be honest, I'm still a bit mystified about how and why it ended up there.

I've always enjoyed thinking about, playing and practising golf, and the design of courses has been a particular interest of mine. As a child growing up in

Bella Hristova, 2007 competition winner, performing at the Winners' Tour recital in 2008 at The Hills clubhouse.

Whangarei, as mentioned earlier, I set up a little miniature course around my parents' house, and charged my schoolmates to play on it. When we moved to Queensland, our home was in a golfing resort, Sanctuary Cove, and upon moving home to the beautiful ski resort of Queenstown, I found the nearest golf course, Millbrook, was all the way across the road.

I suppose I was just used to having a golf course at the back door and in the absence of finding one there, put one in. The silly thing is that although I enjoy golf, it's not really my favourite pastime. I'd rather go fishing or play the violin.

But one morning at our home in Arrowtown, near Queenstown, I looked out the window and thought, 'It would be quite nice to have a putting green.' Two friends, Paddy Baxter and John Darby, designed a green for outside the dining room — and I liked it so much I thought it would be nice to have another, and then another. So, without really meaning to, I ended up with three greens and several bunkers, all around the house.

In 1997 we had a little golf tournament to raise money for Raleigh International, a youth development charity. The idea was that competitors would play 18 holes at Millbrook, then come to Hillbrook, as we then called it, for a shoot-out. New Zealand-born golfer Philip Tataurangi won it one year, then television host Mike Hosking another — it was great fun, and we raised several hundred thousand dollars for Raleigh International.

Which is why I felt slightly miffed when Mike Hosking referred to it as a 'chip and putt' on the television because I know what a chip and putt looks like. I had one in Mann Street in Whangarei in 1949, which did not require a lot of soiling or raking or getting little diggers to put in bunkers.

I thought, I'll show you. We'll put in a proper golf hole.

Are you seeing a pattern forming here? Yep, before long

Our pink house with its three golf holes, the setting for the charity shootout for Raleigh International, 1999.

I had not one hole, but two. Then I thought it may as well have sixteen more.

Business was good and although the estimated cost of building an 18-hole course seemed quite high, I rationalised it with the knowledge that I never waste money. I fly economy on short trips, drink only a small amount of wine, rarely eat out and don't own a holiday home.

So why not?

I'd had so much fun building the first three holes that I thought the next 16 would be the same — but it turned out to be a rather complicated business. After buying our own digger and bulldozer, we had to take the top two metres of soil away and store it, then shape the fairway and form the bunkers and the greens, plus the drainage, the irrigation, the sand, the

The Hills seventeenth hole, 'the Canyons'.

gravel, the seed, the 20,000 tussock plants, the rabbit extermination; the list goes on and on.

To irrigate the 100 hectares of land our golf course covers, we needed to be able to squirt water from one side of the property to the other, which required a massive pump to be placed in a spot known as Dragonfly Lake. Guess what? The digger struck a spring, which turned the whole affair into a wet, muddy nightmare, which could only be contained with a concrete retaining wall.

Building the golf course required six and a half years of earthworks.

But we carried on: earthworks, giant scraping machines, trucks, and more and more mud.

'Gosh, this is costing rather a lot,' Christine said at one point. Ah, yes. The money was haemorrhaging away, but we couldn't really stop. The sixteenth and seventeenth holes took three months of heavy, soggy, dirty, boggy earthmoving; the grounds looked like the battlefields of World War Two.

Did I wish I hadn't started? No, it was exciting and challenging — which is good, because it took six and a half years and ran way over budget.

We did discover an amazing canyon on the property in the process, however. Our designer, John Darby, was walking across a hill one day and said, 'I think there might be a canyon down there.' So we dug and dug and dug, and turned it into the most spectacular hole on the course. The rock took quite a bit of exposing and at one stage I was spending a lot

Top: The Michael Hill New Zealand Open, 2007.
Bottom: The clubhouse structure is set into the hillside, with a lot of it underground, and a grass roof. The main function room overlooks the eighteenth green. Designed by Andrew Patterson of Auckland and built by the Rogers Brothers of Queenstown, it won the supreme award for architecture in New Zealand, and was voted one of the top six sports buildings of the *world* in Barcelona in 2008 — a great thrill!

of time out there myself with a high-pressure hose getting rid of the dirt. People would ring the house to speak to me and Christine would say: 'I'm sorry, Michael can't come to the phone, he is waterblasting his canyon.'

When the course was finished, we needed a clubhouse, otherwise nobody would ever be able to come and enjoy the course. Yes, you guessed it — the cost and time blew out a little. We'd set a budget for the clubhouse, and were very firm that this figure would be the absolute maximum. We ended up with a wonderfully innovative, sustainable, eco-friendly building, where you can stand on the roof and hit a ball onto the course. It's an architectural beauty.

New Zealand golfing icon Bob Charles, who had designed the neighbouring Millbrook course, came over to play a round.

'It's one of the best courses in New Zealand,' Bob said. 'Every bit as good as Cape Kidnappers or Kauri Cliffs. Why don't you host the New Zealand Open?'

He suggested the same thing to the New Zealand Golf Council, who also thought it was a great idea. It all came to fruition — and we now have hosted two New Zealand Golf Open events.

When the tournament began, we had 30,000 spectators on the course, superb weather, and sensational golf. The crowds were wonderfully respectful; after the competition there was not a single piece of litter left on the course.

We staged a dramatic closing ceremony — the most amazing, moving experience. And in that moment it was all worth it. It was beamed out live to 220 million international television viewers, and every day somebody I meet mentions the New Zealand Open. We get calls from golfers all around the world wanting to come and play here.

Those moments made all the expense and drama worthwhile.

From the instant I seriously considered hosting the New Zealand Open I had visualised it being a raging success — why would I visualise anything less?

Michael Hill staff story: Sam Gent
Manager, The Hills, Queenstown

I was born in working-class London, and moved with my musician husband David Gent from The Exponents to Arrowtown, New Zealand, where good core values still exist. This has taken my young family on an amazing journey, with lots of good and bad, which is all part of the process of life. I have owned my own businesses since I was 26 and I've also brought up two lovely boys, now 12 and 15 years old. I'm a very proud mum and they are my first priority.

I met Michael and Christine as clients at my spa and was asked to help design the clubhouse spa rooms. They then asked me to join The Hills course — however, I declined as I believed that the whole business should work together, that is the spa, golf course, and food and beverage under one umbrella. But they wouldn't take no for an answer.

To cut a long story short I now run The Hills and all that that entails, from the clubhouse, golf, the Open and other big-picture development projects, to Michael's everyday doings. Never a dull moment here!

I have an amazing relationship with the Hill family for many reasons. They treat everyone with respect and I really enjoy my life here. My job allows me to do many things in a 'think outside the square and keep it simple' way, which is easily said but hard to do sometimes. The Hills is a unique place where magic happens and is experienced by all. Michael inspires by example, he is always starting new projects, questioning existing business models, wringing the best from staff and expecting more. Some people don't like the constant change and challenge that comes with working for the Hills, but I feel the ones who embrace this philosphy will incorporate it into their own businesses and personal lives and benefit profusely.

Michael challenges me all the time — whenever I think I have it sorted he raises the bar and expects brilliance, so we try harder and we laugh, learn, argue and enjoy ourselves the process. The key for me is: it's okay to try something different and it's essential to be able to critique yourself and always look for better ways of doing things, allowing for creativity and growth. Believe and be fearless in every part of your life and you'll find that everything is possible.

Violin competition staff story: Anne Rodda
Director, New Zealand

It all started at a gig in Taranaki. I was there playing a concert with violinist Miranda Adams, who mentioned in the car on the way back to Auckland that she had just performed with Michael Hill in Gibbston Valley's cave and that he had mentioned to her that he wanted to have a violin competition.

My job at the time was administrating artistic activities for the Auckland Philharmonia Orchestra. We arranged a meeting with Michael Hill and I have to confess that I had assumed the violin competition would be a national event, but he and Christine made it clear from the very beginning that this was to be a major international competition — but one that Kiwis could aspire to, compete in and win.

The best thing about working with Michael on the competition is that he has really left the artistic matters to me, but has put considerable muscle into sponsorship and advertising which are really his strong points. Christine is a trustee and is really a rudder for steady and clear-headed decision-making.

So many artistic endeavours never really take off because

Anne Rodda and me playing in Queenstown to
raise money for our competition, August 2001.

they are inadequately resourced and the corners are cut too much, affecting the original goal. But a lack of this is what has set the violin competition apart in New Zealand — Michael and Christine's vision and generosity have allowed us to get it right from the outset. And from there we have grown from strength to strength and are now on a par with the few other renowned violin competitions in the world.

Michael constantly inspires me to think outside the box and my challenge is to balance trendsetting ideas with the typically staid tradition of classical music. The very fact the competition is held in Queenstown and Auckland provides a freshness to an industry that is normally located in grey, industrial cities.

Violin competition staff story: Dene Olding
Artistic advisor

It is a rare privilege to be asked to help design an international violin competition, and by doing so create a unique event that will encourage the continuation of the glorious tradition of violin playing. I have strived to create a violinistic challenge that reflects the state of violin playing in the world today and cultivates the skills I believe are necessary for a successful career at the highest level.

The outstanding attribute of this competition is that a special atmosphere exists that conveys to the participants empathy, friendship and appreciation of their talents by both judges and the New Zealand public. This has been a feature of the Michael Hill International Violin Competition since its inception and one that has been fostered by the efforts of the generous benefactors behind the event, Michael and Christine Hill. This competition, held amidst the stunning natural beauty of New Zealand, inspires the finest performances from each participant and provides an enjoyable experience for judges and competitors alike.

The virtuoso of today and tomorrow must exhibit outstanding

technical prowess and an individual artistry and be enlightened in their approach to all different musical styles. In addition, they must be completely at ease in all musical situations from concerto performance to chamber music. This competition strives to develop all these skills.

International violin competitions are judged by the quality of the competitors, the quality and integrity of their judges, and the administration and organisation of the event itself. We have been fortunate to have had many distinguished judges serve on the panel since this event was launched. The members of the prestigious judging panel are all highly accomplished performers, teachers and competition winners in their own right, and they bring a variety of backgrounds and musical traditions to New Zealand.

Judges that have served on this panel include Pierre Amoyal, Pamela Frank, Dong Suk Kang, Mark Kaplan, Boris Kuschnir, Paul Kantor, Dene Olding, Hu Kun, Takako Nishizaki, Justine Cormack and Michael Dauth. First-time judges for 2009 include Radoslaw Szulc, Oleh Krysa and Wilma Smith. We will expand this pool of judges in future years and continue to avail ourselves of the exceptional talent available to us from this list.

The Michael Hill International Violin Competition will continue to evolve in future years to fine tune its programme in order to ensure that the countless hours of preparation each contestant invests in this competition will be useful in their life as a professional musician. Our aim is to nurture the talents of the young generation of violinists and bring to the fore the kind of young virtuosi that will thrive in the modern era.

Only a mediocre person is
always at his best.

W Somerset Maugham

Chapter 15

FIND YOUR POINT OF
DIFFERENCE

Jewellery was frightfully conservative when we first started our own business. Though clothing in the 1970s was edgy and energetic, and furniture design was sensationally modern and interesting, for some reason the middle-market jewellery trade seemed trapped in a bygone era.

There was very little interesting or original thinking about how to manufacture, display or sell jewellery. Everybody just set out their wares in neat rows inside ultra-conservative showcases. The staff stood behind the counter waiting for the buyers. And the customers came dutifully trooping in, perhaps three or four times in their lives, having saved for months or years to buy pieces to mark the big milestones: engagement rings, wedding bands, christening spoons and perhaps the occasional gold necklace for a special birthday.

The established retailers seemed fairly smug and complacent about their place in the world. Nobody was ever going to challenge them. It had been done this way for decades, and nothing was going to change as far as they were concerned. Does it sound a little like your industry — or the industry you're trying to crack into?

Well, here's what I learned: it was not an impenetrable fortress. It was exactly the opposite. It was a field of glorious opportunity.

From the outside, an established industry can seem terribly intimidating to a start-up. How on earth can a new enterprise ever get going? Isn't it impossible to change the habits of generations? And if things have always been done this way, how on earth do you set about making a difference, especially when the financial world is about to collapse in on itself.

Our experience, I believe, has showed how it is truly possible for a cheeky new business to conquer a settled, established industry. We changed the business of retailing jewellery dramatically, within a relatively short space of time. And we did that simply by being ourselves, by being different.

As it turned out, things were stable and solid not because the industry players had discovered the perfect way to do everything, but because nobody had ever been bold enough to challenge the accepted wisdom. Customers accepted the indifference and snobbery of most sales staff because nobody offered them anything different. They were used to being treated with relative disdain by most of the industry, which is why my father Dickie — with his charming aptitude for sales, courtesy and genuine interest in the consumer — was such a refreshingly independent character. He was an oddity in the pre-1970s jewellery industry.

What we did was take Dickie's philosophies and turn them into a business: everybody in our stores sold jewellery Dickie's way. But beyond that, we took a fundamentally different approach to the whole thing.

Our stores were modern and fresh. Our windows were eye-catching. Our stock was always immaculately presented. And our approach to pricing was unlike anything the customers had seen. We used loss-leaders.

So how did we do all this? And how exactly do you apply this to your own situation?

Work out what makes you different. By doing your research, you can get to know the industry in which you work, or the industry you're hoping to conquer, in intimate detail. If you don't already work in the trade, find a job with an established player and assess the industry from the inside. Then, sit down and carefully examine everything you've learned. Where are the strengths of the current industry? Where are the weaknesses? And how could things be done differently? If you can see a chink in the wall — a way in which things can be done better — you're halfway there.

Change is often something we fear. It's a natural human tendency; we're creatures of habit, easily spooked. Right now, the world is filled with nervous people in dynamic industries, worrying about their futures.

'Everything's changing,' they fret. 'What's going to happen to my company, my colleagues, my job?'

But economic and global change are terribly exciting, if only you're able to embrace them. And if you think about it logically, that's the only sensible approach. You can't stop the tide turning. But you can make sure you're surfing the wave. Just get out there and paddle like hell.

'Hello, Michael Hill, jeweller.'

That simple introduction, thanks to the magic of television, changed our lives.

Hello, Michael Hill, jeweller.

Without ever intending to, I became a celebrity in Australia and New Zealand within just a few years of starting my own business. That catchphrase was one of the most famous slogans in Australasia. Complete strangers would approach me in the street and shout the phrase at me — and still do. And it was all the result of thinking about how we could do things a little differently.

As the business expanded, we gave a great deal of thought to the idea of expanding from print advertising into the electronic media. I'd begun voicing radio advertisements and thoroughly enjoyed doing them, even singing little songs about our sales and promotions from time to time.

But television seemed too expensive. Buying time on New Zealand's only television station, TVNZ, which broadcast around the country, was prohibitively pricey — and so was hiring a production company to make ads for us.

But shortly after we began trading, a regional television station began in Palmerston North, rebroadcasting the TVNZ signal to a local audience. This meant they could run ads at a much lower price. It also meant less pressure: because the ads weren't going to be seen by a nationwide audience, the stakes weren't quite so high and they could be a little more different and adventurous.

Most television advertising was boring in the early 1980s. Businesses generally hired production companies to make ads according to one of a few standard formats — usually a series of pictures of the goods for sale, backed by a plinkety-plonkety musical jingle and a voice-over explaining all the details. Businesspeople never appeared in their own ads. The ad industry was full of wealthy men in suits who told clients how things were going to be, not the other way around. As a result, everything was formal and stiff.

That was never going to fly with our unconventional style. Had I any idea about how infamous my name and face would become, I would have stuck with my instincts and got another employee — or a professional voice artist — to narrate our advertisements. But at the time, it seemed like a good idea for me to continue doing the advertising like I'd done while working at my uncle's jewellery store.

Radio was pretty staid and frumpy, too, in those days — but in the 1970s it all began to change with the advent of pirate radio. A rebel station, Radio Hauraki, began broadcasting from a ship in the beautiful Hauraki Gulf off Auckland. They were irreverent and clever, and more than willing to do things a little differently. So we got together and produced a series of cutting-edge radio ads, including that jingle: 'Before he proposes and you order the roses, go to Fishers. Fishers the fabulous jewellers, where a diamond ring is a fabulous thing.'

It worked beautifully.

The ad also declared that if anyone wanted an after-hours appointment, 'Mike Hill will come down on his jet-propelled skateboard and open up the shop.' On Radio Northland, the

IT'S ALL OVER

one sterling silver locket worth $15 now $5; ten sterling silver signet rings worth $22 now $9; twenty pairs creole earrings worth $40 now $19; one sterling silver fob chain worth $68 now $29; one ladies bracelet dress watch worth $135 now $69; one 9ct emerald and diamond deternity ring worth $337 now $199; one 9ct gold figaro chain worth $482 now $185; one 9ct gold ruby and diamond cluster worth $449 now $225; one 9ct gold sapphire and diamond three ring set worth $1400 now $599; one 9ct gold curb bracelet with padlock worth $1935 now.$995 etc. etc. Specials available from 9.00am. Thursday one super special per customer Shop 149 B Myer Centre, Queen Street Mall. Stocktaking sale ends Saturday.

Through radio and quirky full-page advertisements in the newspapers we were establishing a serious profile.

local station, I did a similar advertisement, voicing the ad myself. I became great friends with the shopping reporter, Lauraine Rishworth, and she regularly invited me on air to talk retail.

Combined with our use of quirky full-page advertisements in the newspapers, we were establishing a serious profile, and before long Fishers was in the top three jewellery stores for all of New Zealand, by volume of turnover.

So when the possibility of advertising Michael Hill Jeweller on TV came along, we were as keen as could be. Our first television ad was a special promotion to clear a discontinued line of diamond jewellery. I was still a fairly self-conscious fellow at that stage, and was awkward and stiff in front of the camera. In fact, the first ads were absolutely terrible. I was so wooden and stilted, it was embarrassing.

But we had a captive audience. The viewers in Palmerston North only had one channel — and, for some reason, they seemed to think I was amusing. All I did was state my name, my occupation and list the products we were selling. We cleared the diamonds in record time, and before I knew what was happening, the ads had become a cult hit, broadcast around the nation and becoming increasingly slick and professional.

The more the ads worked, the less wooden I became, and we got better and better at making advertisements. We bought in new stock and sold it at big discounts to attract more attention, and the ads became ever more wacky, and I became ever more cheeky.

There was a TV programme at that time called *Private Eye*, featuring puppets lampooning members of the government. They even had a Michael Hill puppet selling jewellery in their 'ad breaks'. You can't pay for advertising like that.

It seemed as if the entire country was saying: 'Hello, Michael Hill, jeweller.'

I went from being a reasonably successful businessman with my name above a few shop doors to being a national celebrity, with a survey in the mid-1980s showing my name and face were as well known as that of the prime minister.

So, suddenly, we had yet another point of difference — innovative marketing. We'd never really set out to become a TV brand; it had just happened through a combination of coincidence and good timing. I wasn't afraid to make a goose of myself on TV in Palmerston North, because I figured it didn't really matter if a few thousand viewers thought I was a bit odd.

But when the ads were so successful and we took them nationwide — then I was making a goose of myself in front of all of New Zealand.

When we moved into the Australian market, it seemed natural to keep going — and now I was to become a trans-Tasman goose. It was too late to pull out. Now that I had a reputation for being a bit of a character, I had to keep fulfilling people's expectations. The ads were to become more and more outlandish as the years went on — and still, everywhere I went people barked, 'Hello, Michael Hill, jeweller' at me.

After setting up in Queensland, we decided to centralise our ad-making facilities, rather than flying all over the place to make different advertisements for both markets. The only studio that could meet our modest budget was in Toowoomba, a smaller regional city about two hours out of Brisbane. Once a month we'd get in the car and make the long drive — Christine would pack a lunch — and spend the day at this tiny TV station in the sticks filming the commercials, then drive back.

The car would be stuffed with costumes and props, most of which Christine had made. For a Christmas sale, we decided I was going to be a Christmoose (did I mention these ads were outlandish?). Christine constructed a moose head out of papier mâché, which looked fantastic — but it was devilishly hot inside that thing.

For another ad, I was painted gold (wearing a suit, I hasten to add). I was the village crier in yet another, then a cowboy. I've been Santa Claus, a scuba-diver — everything you could imagine, and many I've chosen to forget.

While the commercials were pretty ridiculous, I'd reached a stage of confidence about my delivery that meant I actually enjoyed making them. There was no doubt they attracted enormous attention, which was an extra incentive — and even though I took a bit of ribbing, I didn't really care.

The papier mâché
moose head.

Christmooses and cowboys aside, the most memorable ad in the minds of the Australian and New Zealand public, without question, was the one we made for a chain sale. I'd seen an ad for a burger chain that employed a short, repetitive slogan, and I couldn't get it out of my head. I knew if it had struck me so markedly, it would also grab the attention of other consumers, so I borrowed the idea.

'Hello, Michael Hill, jeweller,' I announced in our new ad. Then I began the chant: 'Gold gold silver silver chain chain sale sale.'

Then I said it faster — and faster, and faster.

It haunts me to this day. As it turned out, everyone noticed it. And remembered it. And delighted in repeating it whenever and wherever I appeared.

Being well known in Whangarei was a kick because I knew all the people who knew me, but being a minor celebrity in Brisbane was a whole new experience. Everywhere I went, someone would greet me with 'G'day, Michael Hill!'

That was fine — but the 'chain chain sale sale' changed everything. I remember one day walking from our Brisbane offices down to our main store, and stopping at an intersection where a whole lot of school buses were pulled up. Well, one kid saw me and started chanting 'gold gold silver silver chain chain sale sale.'

Then all his mates joined the chant. The kids on the bus behind heard the commotion and joined in — and so did all the kids on the bus behind that, and the bus behind that. They were yelling out the windows, and everyone in the street was staring. I was mortified. Sure, it was encouraging to see how well our advertising was working, but this had really got beyond being fun. I quickly scuttled into the store and tried to recover my composure before braving the public again.

Advertising was only one of the ways in which we made our business different, but it announced us to the world as an innovative, fresh-thinking brand. It got customers thinking differently about ways they could buy jewellery. Suddenly, they weren't restricted to buying the occasional big-event item from a stodgy, conventional business. Our prices meant that people could buy jewellery for themselves, and for one another, whenever they liked. They could buy it on a whim. And it was high-quality, of original design and displayed and sold with what we always hoped was a sense of care and dedication.

We were lucky, in a way, that the industry was so self-confident and complacent when we first began. There was plenty of room for cheeky troublemakers like ourselves. We've always tried to maintain the mindset of a start-up. We're constantly entering new markets — be they new towns or new countries — and refreshing our approach to make a splash all over again.

And now, we're refreshing the entire brand, with a new look, a new image and a new set of goals. That's why I've no intention of retiring. This can't possibly be work — it's far too much fun.

Setting sail

Ever been on a superyacht?

I hadn't till I stepped aboard my own. And as soon as I walked onto the deck, I had a strange sense of déjà vu. I'd been here before, in my dreams.

Christine and I have spent decades in and around boats. When I was a kid, Billie would row me out fishing out on the Whangarei Harbour in a little wooden dinghy, inspiring the passion for fishing I've had ever since. Christine and I have also loved fishing in our

I've always loved boats and through time they grew bigger and better. From top: *Boston Whaler*, 1972; our bright yellow *Commander Cat*, 1986; a stunning 17-metre game boat, *Amokura*, with a top speed of nearly 40 knots.

little dinghies together over the years. We'd net flounder or catch snapper in the channel, row back home to our rented cottage and cook them.

We slowly upgraded our boats, little by little. First we got an outboard motor for the dinghy, then a slightly bigger boat, a Boston whaler on which we used to take the kids out on Whangarei Harbour when they were small.

It's a miracle the children survived some of those trips. I remember one day when Emma was a toddler and Mark about five, we were fishing just outside the channel. I was feeding a flounder net out the back when I accidentally bumped the outboard motor. The boat suddenly zipped forward, and I went flying out the back of the boat into the sea, while Christine was knocked to the deck. Thankfully, she was able to recover, scramble to the wheel and turn the boat around to collect me. If she'd been knocked overboard as well, I hate to think what would have become of the children.

I've always loved boats, and imagining new and better vessels has always been a favourite part of my goal-setting and visualisation. While living in Australia, we became enamoured of game-fishing. We befriended Bill Edwards, aka 'The Eagle', a legendary Australian skipper and boat-designer who could always spot a fish before it took the bait, and had a knack for finding marlin. He designed us a stunning 17-metre boat, which we named *Amokura*. It was powered by two massive motors, with a top speed of 40 knots, and we had some wonderful trips in Australia around the Gold Coast. Further north, at the legendary Lizard Island, a mecca for game fishermen, I hooked a massive black marlin while trawling off a reef. We explored much of the beautiful New Zealand coastline off *Amokura* too, from the Bay of Islands in the north to Stewart Island down south.

But I had a fancy for something more — and so we commissioned a Canadian designer, Greg Marshall, to build us a large, luxurious vessel on which we could entertain our friends, catch some serious fish and relax in comfort.

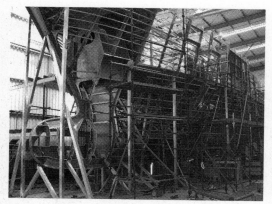

The beginning of constuction of *VvS1*, the first three stories! She was built in the efficient and world-renowned shipyard Alloy Yachts, in Auckland, New Zealand.

I'd visualised the boat from bow to stern before we ever put pen to paper, imagining us stepping aboard, walking through the galley, feeling the wooden decks under my feet.

She was to be a super-yacht, but we had no interest in anchoring off Monaco and frolicking around with the A-list like the superyacht owners you read about in magazines — we just wanted to have a comfortable exploration vessel.

When you love food and entertaining as much as we do, the design of a boat — or a house — is all about the kitchen. We didn't want a typical galley stuck in the dark, steamy bowels of the boat, so we asked Greg to put the galley at the aft of the vessel, with a view of the sea and open serving hatches to indoor and outdoor dining spaces. It fitted the mood we were after — convivial, casual dining where our crew members could talk to us and our guests, enjoying the fresh air and the relaxed, fun atmosphere we like.

Our crew members are our friends, so we don't want them hidden away, suffocating in the dark while we enjoy the sunshine. All our crew have worked on superyachts around the world, and we respect their skills enormously. Naturally, we treat them just as we would any staff members; they are our co-adventurers and equals.

On the main deck we added a library, a main double bedroom — including a bathtub — and below decks we added three double cabins for friends, and crew cabins, galley and mess. Upstairs, a clever floating staircase leads to the bridge and captain's double

VvS1 is a jewellery term that refers to an almost-flawless diamond. True to the name, she won the world superyacht award for her class.

bedroom, a decent gym (as I hate being inactive on a boat) and a family room.

Like everything else I've been involved in designing, it kept growing: from 22 to 34 metres. We loved the design process, however; envisaging what we wanted, and watching it take shape on the plans, was thrilling. We added two runabouts for fishing and zipping in to shore for supplies, and a flybridge above the top deck with a teppanyaki bar to seat 10 diners, as well as a barbecue and lounge area.

Christine and Monika, our daughter-in-law, chose colours of dark grey and metallic silver, and the boat looks almost like a battleship — it has quite a military, functional look. It certainly attracts a lot of attention. We've spent quite a bit of time up in the Bay of Islands and often watch people row out from the shore and do a lap of us to check out the boat. If she wasn't mine, I would too.

Her name, *VvS1*, is a jewellery term that refers to an almost-flawless diamond. The initials stand for very, very slightly included — that is, very, very slightly flawed. Only an expert can detect flaws in a VvS1 diamond with a 10-magnification jeweller's loop glass.

Why didn't we call the superyacht 'Flawless'? Well, here's another thing I have learned in life: nothing is perfect. That's what keeps you striving for more.

Don't hold the dime so near
your eye that you can't see
the dollar.
Anonymous

Chapter 16

MONEY IS JUST A YARDSTICK

A few years ago, Christine jumped in a taxi and asked the driver to head for the nearest Michael Hill store.

'So you work for Michael Hill, do you?' asked the cabbie. 'What exactly do you do there?

'Oh, this and that. You know, a bit of everything,' Christine said. She just didn't have the energy for the conversation she knew was about to unfold.

The driver looked at her quizzically. Christine sighed — she was going to have to come clean.

'I'm Michael's wife,' she said.

The cabbie turned to stare in astonishment. 'Really?' he said. 'You're Mrs Hill?'

He seemed somehow disappointed.

'But . . . you just don't look like what I'd have thought you would.'

Christine gritted her teeth, smiling as politely as possible. She's had this conversation many times over the years, and in her down-to-earth Yorkshire way, she's decidedly over it.

'What were you expecting?' she said. 'A tiara?'

Christine doesn't wear a lot of jewellery, much as some people expect her to. It simply isn't her style. She has a few beautiful pieces, which she enjoys — but she's never glittering with bling, and she's never been anywhere near a tiara.

Our first $100,000 had to be earned, squirreled away to get us started. But after we had three stores, our focus changed. Money was now a yardstick, rather than a goal. Our ambitions have always been about far more interesting things — the satisfaction of owning our own jewellery chain, the excitement of exploring new lands, the challenge of resolving problems, and the satisfaction of doing things that some consider impossible. We only ever use money as a way to measure our success. As a yardstick, it is tremendously useful: it's an instant, easily grasped encapsulation of how things are going.

Whenever we hear our turnover figures are higher, it's great because it means we can start dreaming up our next adventure. Solid earnings mean we can hire more people, foster more careers, encourage more entrepreneurs within our own organisation, and help them develop the skills to make their own private dreams fly.

That, to us, is what it's all about. And that's why we keep expanding. Our attitude has always been that if we're having a blast doing this, we'd love to share it with more people, and really soar together.

Our goal has never been to make a certain amount of

money by a certain time. That's no fun at all. What do you do once you've climbed that mountain — sit around and count your cash? I can't think of anything more dull.

But money isn't just boring. It can be dangerous. We all know the stories of people who become obsessive about work. I think often they are simply consumed by greed, by the unthinking urge to accumulate more and more, ever-ballooning piles of stuff. And once you have a lot of stuff — be it houses or racehorses or shares or whatever — you need more and more money to keep it all. And then you're trapped, a prisoner to the things you've accumulated.

I would like to think that Christine and I have been able to use money for good. As well as employing a lot of wonderful people in interesting and creative jobs, we give substantial amounts to charitable ventures, operate a world-class violin competition, run a golf tournament for the world's top players and, hopefully, bring pleasure to a few of our fellow citizens along the way. I love watching the crowds of spectators at the New Zealand Open, and it's a huge thrill to see a talented young musician bask in the applause of an audience.

I think there's a lot of curiosity about what it's like to be rich and the truth is, it's quite handy. We have a superyacht, for example. But to be honest with you, we didn't commission the yacht because we wanted to show off. We commissioned it because we thought it might be fun to design. And it was. In fact, I think we both enjoyed the process of designing and creating the yacht more than we actually enjoy luxuriating on it.

It's great to be able to invite our friends aboard and investigate little hidden bays, or watch dolphins playing around in the pristine waters of New Zealand.

We're also able to help friends, when they need us. We

try to make a difference in people's lives — like the time I loaned my priceless violin to brilliant young violinist Feng Ning. For him, playing on a Stradivarius was an impossible dream. I was able to help make it come true. And that's a great feeling.

When I tell people I've no intention of retiring, I get the impression they sometimes think I'm so money-hungry I just can't get enough, and I can't see that there is more to life than money. On the contrary. I know life is about much, much more. That's why I can't possibly retire — I'm enjoying all the stuff I do so much that I'd be miserable if I stopped. I know myself well enough to know that I'm driven by success. It's an addictive feeling to achieve a goal you've set for yourself. I don't ever want to give up on visualising my dreams and making them happen.

For me, success is about making our business grow in a way that will create the greatest amount of benefit for our people. For someone else, it might be losing a stack of weight, or building a house from the ground up. And that's so, so much more important than how much you've got in the bank.

Christine and I are still very money-conscious. I'd estimate we have saved thousands of dollars — if not hundreds of thousands — over the years by eating the packed lunches she has always made for us. At first, we ate home-made because we couldn't afford to eat out. Then we continued because it seemed crazy to spend $30 on a few sandwiches and a couple of drinks if we could eat something much tastier and healthier for a few dollars. And now it's almost a point of pride. Underneath all the apparent trappings of wealth, we still live by the principles of her working-class English parents, and my careful mother Billie, who started my very first bank account when I was a tiny boy, and was as delighted as I was in seeing the balance grow.

Back in the Whangarei days, I brewed my own beer to save money. I did it for 15 years, and in the end, I made a damn good home brew: seven pounds of malt extract, seven pounds of sugar, seven ounces of hops, a yeast

Whangarei: Me, Mark and a glass of home brew, 1971.

culture and two tablespoons of gravy browning, to give it a lovely dark colour.

We used to make sake in the bath. We grew our own vegetables (and still do), caught and smoked our own fish, and even dined on possum stew. That's how we saved our first $100,000, which was the hardest money to make, of course. Once a business reaches a certain level of turnover and profit, it will often just keep itself going, if you're a competent manager. But the hardscrabble habits of our early years never left us.

And frugality has many unexpected joys. In Whangarei in the 1970s, the local liquor store was selling off the oak barrels in which it imported Coruba rum from Jamaica. In the days of strict alcohol licensing, the over-proof rum had to be watered down to meet the local standards, then bottled and labelled. My mate Alan Spicer and I thought the barrels would make good flower pots. So we bought the lot, aiming to cut them in half and sell them.

When we sawed them in half, there was quite a lot of over-proof rum still sloshing around. Someone at the liquor store hadn't bothered to empty them carefully, and we extracted about 100 flagons of the most delicious, super-intense Jamaican liquid gold. It kept us going for years. It would blow your socks off, mind you, and take your eyebrows with them if anyone lit a match. We made good money selling the flower pots too.

I occasionally fly business class, but only on long-haul flights. The rest of our team, including Emma, always flies economy and so do Christine and I when we're only taking a short trip. And I'm never too shy to ask for an upgrade at the check-in desk, which embarrasses Christine enormously. Why not, I always reason — I try to negotiate everything at a better price. Everything.

Most of my investments create more wealth. I have my assets like the golf course and the boat, but I also have a share portfolio which I pay someone else whom I trust implicitly to manage because I know nothing about the sharemarket — in fact, I don't know that anyone knows much about the sharemarket any more.

Although we're big charitable spenders, we have to be careful because we're often asked for money by complete strangers. People just ring the house and ask for it, like the lady who told Christine she'd lost her wallet and asked for $500. We'd rather give to causes that will benefit the broader society in some way.

Of course, all the money in the world is nothing if you can't share it with the people you love. I'm lucky to have the wonderful, direct, loyal, loving Christine as my partner in life and in business. She is open and honest, a realist who knows exactly when and how to tell me I'm being crazy — and when to support my dreams.

We have our independence; Christine spends a great deal

of time working on her amazing art. But we also spend a great deal of time together. She goes wherever I go; I'd never go out drinking with the boys and leave her at home. I think that's part of the secret of a good marriage; we love one another's company. I'm enormously grateful for her support, and she has taught me that a brilliant partner can be crucial to achieving any kind of success.

I certainly couldn't have done it without her, and I hope you're lucky enough to have a partner who supports your endeavours. It's very hard to succeed if the people closest to you are negative or doubting, and if that is the case in your life, perhaps it's time to apply some clear, focused thinking to your relationships. Visualise the sort of partnership you'd really love to have — and then think about how you can make it happen. By investing some of your time in protecting and nurturing your relationship, you'll make your whole life better, and set yourself up for success.

I'm extraordinarily lucky now to have my family all around. Mark and his wife Monika live close by, as do Emma and her husband Doug, as well as all our grandchildren: Nathan, Oliver, Chloe and Jacob. Our kids are our best friends, and I

Mark is a sculpture artist and works in welded steel. Here he is with his 'Welcoming Party' sculpture, which is being blessed by a local Maori elder at Queenstown Airport, November 2006.

At Emma and Doug's wedding, from left: Mark, Monika, Oliver, Nathan, me, Christine, Emma and Doug. Not pictured are the latest arrivals — twins, Chloe and Jacob.

enjoy their company more than anyone else's.

But we've had to work on making the connections work between our family and our business. A while ago Wayne Peters, who is on our board, suggested we start having twice-yearly family meetings, which have been enormously beneficial. We have a formal agenda and catch up on everyone's goals, projects and opinions on the family's many ventures — the boat, the golf course, home sites and plans for the future — as well as any personal issues. We often have someone outside of the family chair the meeting.

We were hard on our kids financially as they grew up; we wanted them to develop their own gradual success, and learn along the way. They did all that, and more, and I'm enormously proud.

There's no secret to my success. All I needed was to find out what I really wanted from life. My house burnt to the ground, and I was jolted into the realisation that would change me for ever.

And once I had my vision, I had to find the people I needed to make it come true — people I could trust to be my co-conspirators and my anchors. Then I had to go away and let them get on with it, so I could dream up what I wanted next.

From the self-conscious, shy child I once was, I've grown enormously. Today, I have total faith in myself, in the people around me and in the endless possibilities of the universe. I think up a goal, work out how to achieve it and then believe with all my being that it will come true. It usually does.

But I could still be working behind the counter of someone else's jewellery shop. I hope you don't need a house fire to shock you into finding your own destiny; it's a rather traumatic way to learn a lesson.

If my story proves anything, I hope it is this: it is never too late to find your dream. And you — only you — can make it a reality.

Have a wonderful adventure.

If you have
what it takes
to be a winner,
I want to hear
from you.

michael hill

Contact us on

michaelhill.com

Michael Hill